JIMM

Foreword by Internat...
Clifton L. Taulbert

EQUIPPED
—— TO ——
SERVE

Empowered People, Empower Others

Hart Global Industries, LLC

Equipped to Serve
Empowered People, Empower Others
All Rights Reserved.
Copyright © 2023 Jimmy D. Hart
v3.0

The opinions expressed in this manuscript are solely the opinions of the author and do not represent the opinions or thoughts of the publisher. The author has represented and warranted full ownership and/or legal right to publish all the materials in this book.

This book may not be reproduced, transmitted, or stored in whole or in part by any means, including graphic, electronic, or mechanical without the express written consent of the publisher except in the case of brief quotations embodied in critical articles and reviews.

Hart Global Industries, LLC

ISBN: 978-0-578-27755-4

Cover Photo © 2023 KieferPix/Shutterstock.com. All rights reserved - used with permission.
Cover Design: Alaka Basit

PRINTED IN THE UNITED STATES OF AMERICA

DEDICATION

This book is dedicated to every person who felt they were powerless. You are not powerless, you are powerful. To everyone who has a desire to make our world a better place, I dedicate this book to you. To all who empower others, keep on empowering. Empowered people, empower people.

To my ancestors, thank you.

ACKNOWLEDGEMENT

Thank you to:

Desiree Cook, you empower with humility and gratefulness.

Margaret Hart, you are quality-time – I get it – thank you.

Fred and Tiffany Lux, your unselfishness is life changing.

Trehon Cockrell-Coleman, keep inspiring others, we need it.

Sabrina Mejia, your positivity is contagious.

Regina Hart, your people-centered heart is extremely unselfish.

Dwight Hart, your example will continue to live for generations to come.

Clifton L. Taulbert, thank you for developing others – your legacy will continue.

I thank my family for their continued support of my work. To my wife Regina, thank you for your motivation and being an amazing teammate. To my son Joshua, and daughter Jordan, thank you for letting me be Dad. To my siblings, thank you for encouragement. To my parents, thank you for your love. To our men's zoom bible study group, thank you for your push to finish. To Almighty God, thank you.

Table of Contents

About the Author: Jimmy Hart i

Foreword: The Young Educator... On a Mission then and Now. . . . iii

Introduction: Equipped to Serve Workbook. ix

Chapter 1: **E**mpower Others 1

Chapter 2: **Q**uality Time With Others 9

Chapter 3: **U**nselfishness Towards Others. 18

Chapter 4: **I**nspire Others 30

Chapter 5: **P**ositive Attitude Towards Others 38

Chapter 6: **P**eople-Centered Towards Others 48

Chapter 7: **E**xample For Others 58

Chapter 8: **D**evelop Others 65

Chapter 9: Kindness: The X-Factor 74

Chapter 10: Who We Serve 79

Final Thoughts. 89

Equipped to Serve Self-Assessment. 91

Endnotes 93

ABOUT THE AUTHOR

Jimmy Hart

JIMMY D. HART serves as an author, coach, mentor, speaker, and trainer devoted to building people up and working with organizations to improve how they serve and support each other. He has spent the last 40 years serving people of all ages and backgrounds in the areas of education, leadership, and personal development. Growing up with parents who taught and volunteered as tutors and mentors in their community, his first experience serving others was at age 12 working with struggling readers. That experience helped to shape his life work of serving and helping others to achieve their goals. Having completed his master's degree and Ed.S. degree, his work to build leaders and coach adults began in 2000.

He worked as a middle and high school teacher for 7 years, worked in career education and dropout prevention, served as a middle and high school leader for 10 years, and as a district leader for 13 years. Through life experiences, family, work, and education, he has found life changing value in living out the principles outlined in Equipped to Serve: Empowered People, Empower Others. Serving as a coach and mentor, he has helped others in his community and nation to live empowered lives. His work as an educator has provided opportunities to speak and provide training on issues of community and diversity for over 25 years to thousands of college students, educators, businesses, service providers, and community leaders.

Jimmy is identified as a leader who exemplifies the timeless character attribute of Hope by internationally recognized author, Clifton L. Taulbert, and has received numerous awards for his work as an educator and leader. He was honored by the local service chapter of the National Exchange Club, received the Southern Arizona 25 Most Influential African Americans award, and honored as an unsung hero by the Women's Progressive and Civic Club in his hometown. He continues to serve his community by volunteering on local and state boards for K12 education and higher education.

Jimmy is president of Hart Global Industries and is happily married to his wife Regina with whom he has two young adult children.

FOREWORD

THE YOUNG EDUCATOR... ON A MISSION THEN AND NOW

IT WAS ALMOST two decades ago when I first saw Jimmy Hart, and I still remember that day. He moved with such quickness and agility through the hallways that it totally caught my attention. I tried to imagine his agenda as I kept my eyes focused on the hallway which was right outside the auditorium where I was seated waiting my turn to speak. And just about my time to walk to the podium, the young African American male whizzed through the side of the room as if he were on a mission that demanded his total self. I finally asked the person sitting next to me who also worked at the same school...the identity of the mission focused young man. The lady smiled as if I was the hundredth person asking that same question. With co-worker pride, she did not hesitate to respond. "That's Mr. Hart...Jimmy Hart."

That morning is forever imprinted on my brain—a man on a mission. His reputation for professionalism was obvious in the way he moved with purpose. I would learn from his co-worker of his commitment to the young people many of whom had multiple social needs—social needs that would demand his care and commitment. I would learn that he gave both. His reputation among his peers was equally impressive. He was the epitome of a team player as was told to me by his peers. I could not wait to meet him. He was indeed a bright light in an environment where many had almost thrown up their hands. Educating had changed on so many fronts and so had the social ills within many of the students' communities. Apparently, this Mr. Hart, also an athlete, simply said through his actions, "Throw Me the Ball."

I had given my talk on the "Eight Habits of the Heart" and how ordinary people whose lives had been lived out on the Mississippi Delta during the era of legal segregation had become extraordinary leaders on my behalf. For me, they were the "Eight Habits of the Heart—Nurturing Attitude, Responsibility, Dependability, Friendship, Sisterhood-Brotherhood, High Expectations, Courage, and Hope. Their unselfishness had transformed my life and if embraced within our schools, school communities could also be transformed. Little did I know that Mr. Hart had stood near the entrance to the auditorium and had heard my speech. He even took notes. After finishing my talk, I was granted my request and was introduced to the young educator. We were introduced. We shook Hands. I stood and waited and then Mr. Hart just blurted out, "WOW! Those habits were awesome." From that unexpected crossing of paths, a mentorship would develop and one that continues years later. I knew intuitively that young Mr. Hart was on a mission and that educators, parents and students would benefit from his commitment to do all he could to see the lives of the students under his watch and the peers with whom he worked fully maximized.

I am honored that the next chapter in this educator's life will include all that he has learned, implemented, and shared with his peers.

IV

Jimmy Hart has served the nation in these academic capacities: He has served as a middle school teacher and from there to being an assistant principal for both middle school and high school. Jimmy has also served his students and peers as assistant director of a large comprehensive technology center. Mr. Hart's educational journey continued as high school principal and becoming a district director for student services. His over thirty-year educational career has clearly exemplified that of the Servant Leader. For him, the success of others matters.

Much of the work and training I have been privileged to deliver around the world will be extended through Jimmy Hart - and this book now in your hands will give you insight on his continued commitment to academic excellence and the power of the "Eight Habits of the Heart" to transform lives. His mission hasn't changed. When I first met him many years ago, I felt that this man will indeed touch our Nation through education – the students he meets and the educators whose paths he will cross. Indeed, he has, and the mission continues.

I am honored to have been asked to write the Foreword to EQUIPPED TO SERVE: Empowered People, Empower Others.

Clifton L. Taulbert
Entrepreneur, Pulitzer Nominee, International Lecturer
Eight Habits of the Heart for Educators
Once Upon a Time When We Were Colored
The invitation
Who Owns the Icehouse
The Last Train North

INTRODUCTION

"Those who are happiest are those who do the most for others."[1]
– Booker T. Washington

SERVING OTHERS IS a communal practice, to serve our neighbor, serve our community and country, and serve our families. Serving others is in our DNA make-up.

Although service is an intrinsic part of who we are as humans, it often falls to the wayside. In this book, I extend an opportunity and challenge to all of us as a human race to be better. This book is for anyone wanting to be of greater service to their family, friends, community, and world. I offer the opportunity to reflect on how each of us, as unique individuals, can serve others through timeless principles. Because you are reading this, I encourage you to grow in service, grow in your thinking, and serve as an ambassador to promote ideas that honor the value in serving others.

Equipped to Serve shares eight timeless principles to live empowered lives within our home and community. However, to grow as individuals and as a community, we must constantly grow in our self-reflection and understanding of how we can make this world we live in

VII

a better place. According to John Maxwell, "to become a better human being, you need to grow in character." *Equipped to Serve: Empowered People, Empower Others* is designed to empower readers to grow in their personal relationships, grow in their work relationships, grow as an influencer in their community, and grow in their relationships as a parent, sibling, or child – even as an adult child engaging with your parent(s).

To serve is to help someone and to put others' needs before yours. Equipped means we have the necessary tools to complete a particular task. When you put both words together, being equipped to serve refers to having the necessary tools to help someone else in need. During our time together in this book, I will highlight the tools we already have access to at no cost to better serve others.

Martin L. King, Jr. proclaimed, "Everybody can be great because everybody can serve. You don't have to have a college degree to serve. You don't have to make your subject and your verb agree to serve. You only need a heart full of grace, a soul generated by love." Dr. King would also share, "Life's most persistent and urgent question is: What are you doing for others?"

Equipped to serve is divided into two sections. The first nine chapters articulate how we serve – and give ideas, principles, and strategies on how everyone can serve. Service is not just for the company president, church pastor, or school principal. Service is not only for the school-aged student working on a service project, but for everyone. Within each chapter, I highlight individuals from history to present-day ordinary people living out the principles outlined in this book. Be encouraged by the life stories of everyday people, and I encourage you to take the necessary time to engage in completing the self-reflection activities at the end of each chapter.

The second section in the book defines who we serve – who we serve is designed to add perspective to our work as servants, as leaders serving in our community, and as servants in our homes. We must be intentional in our service to others.

The characteristics outlined in this book are not new and have been researched, written about, and discussed for many years. The idea of character traits is not a new topic and is one that has been highlighted by international militaries, world-famous motivational speakers, and scholars. Each characteristic has been discussed by educators and parents alike for centuries. However, they've never been organized in a way to draw attention to the priceless power and ability we have within us to serve others.

By the time you have read and completed the exercises in these pages, you will feel a sense of empowerment knowing that you are equipped to serve others, and that your actions matter. More importantly, you will know and be able to practice strategies to empower others. If you already have a strong sense of self-empowerment, our time together will remind you that you do make a difference and you have the ability to make greater impact in the lives of others.

EQUIPPED TO SERVE WORKBOOK

Download a FREE copy of the Equipped to Serve: Empowered People, Empower Others E-Workbook @ **www.jimmyhartglobal.com**.

CHAPTER 1

EMPOWER OTHERS

EMPOWER OTHERS - Giving others the encouragement, confidence, and tools, they need to succeed in taking control of their own life or circumstances.

Often, we read the word "empower" or "empowerment" and think in terms of those who are in leadership positions. Some may consider the scholarly articles and dissertations that focus on the history and origins of the word empower or empowerment. However, when I discuss empowering others, I hope to bring to light that we all have the ability to do so. We need not be in a specific position of power to empower. Exemplars of empowering others exist all throughout history, and many were not formal leaders. For example, Rosa Parks helped to spark an entire movement to give individuals who were historically marginalized a voice. Mrs. Parks worked as a seamstress and was active in her local NAACP chapter. Her act of not giving up her seat on a bus in Montgomery, Alabama, in 1955 encouraged others to speak-up and have the confidence needed to fight for positive changes in our country. She used her voice and community engagement to empower others positively. It would

1

Equipped to Serve

have been easy for her to continue with the status quo practices of her time. Instead, she took a stand for a better world, and empowered others for years to come.

Author and thought leader, John Maxwell, shares, "The act of empowering others changes lives, and it's a win-win situation for you and the people you empower."[3] In other words, empowering others is beneficial to the recipient and the giver. I agree with John Maxwell's perspective on empowerment. Empowering others creates a type of Synergy. Empowerment moves from one person to another, and to another. Empowered people, empower others. Empowering others has the potential to create dividends well beyond the person or persons you choose to empower. Empowering others creates positive synergy, a sense of positive energy that continues to be passed on. The long-term effects of empowering others can have a lasting impact on future generations. According to Maxwell, "When you empower people, you're not influencing just them; you're influencing all the people they influence. That's impact!"

I know firsthand the power and lasting impact of empowering others. From my second and third grade teachers, Mrs. Summers, and Mrs. Lewis respectively, to my Geometry teacher, Mrs. Taylor, and my Counselors, Mrs. Thomas and Mr. Pinellas, their ability to empower others continues long past their days as educators. They grew up during the era of Rosa Parks and the Civil Rights Movement. As educators, they made it their priority to empower every student, regardless of background, that entered their offices and classrooms. While they did not serve as an executive of a large company, or impact public policy, or serve as the school principal, they were equipped to be encouragers, build confidence in others, and give others the tools they needed to succeed in their circumstances at the time. One of my fondest memories was Mrs. Summers and Mrs. Lewis allowing me the opportunity to take my desk into the hallway and copy the information of famous Americans in history

EMPOWER OTHERS

that was hanging on the walls. As a second and third grader, I was amazed at the historical figures, and the idea that I could be like the people hanging on the walls was uplifting. To know I could be like Langston Hughes, Jackie Robinson, and Benjamin Banneker – men who looked like me was empowering. Mr. Pinellas, my high school counselor, would teach me the importance of P.O.T. – Power Over Temptation, a lesson that I have passed on to the next generation. This lesson is based on the idea that we have the power to make the right choice, even if it's difficult, and avoid the temptation to make a poor choice for immediate gratification, as it would have a long-term negative impact.

Like my teachers and counselors, you don't have to be the company president or person in charge to empower others. Take, for example, my first job in education. I worked for the local Urban League as part of a summer enrichment program for elementary students. The organizers took a risk and hired me as the lead coordinator for their program even though I did not have extensive experience in education. My task would be to help students in grades three through five improve their reading. Ironically, outside of babysitting my two younger brothers, I had never supervised elementary-aged students, let alone taught them to read. My supervisor at the time, a humble woman in her late 40s, would create a sense of empowerment in myself and my two co-workers, who were one year younger than me.

Fortunately for us, she looked beyond our practical experience and focused in on our potential. She was in a position to empower us to do something great. At the start of our summer program, she gave us lots of encouragement, she boosted our confidence with every planning meeting, and she ensured we had the necessary tools to run a successful program. Anyone who has tried homeschooling or teaching elementary-aged students knows that it can be like herding cats if you don't have a plan in place that is engaging. However, for my teammates and me, our supervisor took the time to prepare us to work five days per

3

week for three hours with students ages eight to ten. Without much research or the ability to make national policy changes, she understood the connection between reading and literacy rates, dropout rates, and incarceration in America. She empowered me at 19, and my two teammates who were 18, to run a successful summer reading enrichment program. By empowering us, we, in turn, empowered the group of students, influencing the wider community through higher literacy rates. My supervisor's work would empower and influence three teenagers, who would empower and influence many others.

Fast forward to the present, and because of her initial investment in a group of ambitious teenagers, I have served as an educator for 30 years, and one teammate (also a classmate) has served for 25 years. My classmate has served as a school district superintendent for 15 years, and I've served as a school principal and district leader for over 20 years. You can imagine the number of students and families we've been able to empower through education and services. It all started with a risk-taking supervisor who was willing to empower a group of teenagers. Her efforts exemplify the idea that empowering others has the potential to create dividends well beyond the person or persons you choose to empower.

Another obscure example of empowering others is a lady named Desiree Cook (also identifies as Queen). If you were to run into Desiree in a grocery store you would walk past her. She is unassuming and at most you may be inclined to say hello because she smiled as you walked by. If you were to have a conversation with her, you may learn that she spent time in prison and that she lost everything including her children because of drugs and poor choices. However, her story doesn't stop there, which is why I identify her as someone who truly empowers. Desiree, an obscure woman, working as a hairstylist living in the southwestern part of the United States, decided she was not defined by her past and would live out what it means to empower others. She chose to create a space that gave others encouragement,

EMPOWER OTHERS

confidence, and the tools they need to succeed in taking control of their own life circumstances. Desiree has gone from prison to creating promise and potential for others. She used her life experiences to create a non-profit designed for homeless and foster children. According to the U.S. Department of Health and Human Services, in 2018, approximately 440,000 children were in foster care. When these children turn 18, they have nowhere to go.

Desiree, with little financial support, had a vision to create tiny homes for foster children who had aged out of the foster care system. Her desire to empower others has overtime resulted in national recognition and financial support of her foster care tiny home project. When interviewing her for this book on serving others, she shared the following:

"All the kids in foster care could be my kids. My kids were in foster care while I was in prison and they had to endure the abandonment, lack of trusting adults, and living without their mother. I was fortunate to get my kids back, but I also saw the damage from my behavior, and I wanted to help other children feel empowered and valued like I was able to do for my kids. I want other kids to know they are not alone. Now, all the energy I had put into drug addiction, I put into something positive for generations to come. So many people are losing their homes, so I work to stand up for other people. It was a long road and I had to do a lot of learning and relearning, so I linked up with mentors to do this work. My faith kept developing the vision and giving me hope, so I want to share it with others. I can't be stingy or selfish, and it is necessary for my soul to lift others up. My lived experiences and honoring my truth have given me the ability to be free and to help others with freedom. I believe it's vital for all of us to develop self-awareness to share our strengths with the world. When you empower others, everyone wins."

Empowering others is about having a willingness and commitment to giving those around you the tools they need to succeed. Even a word of encouragement can spark someone to feel empowered. Empowered people, empower others.

> **Empowered People, Empower Others.**

GIVE BACK BY EMPOWERING SOMEONE

Empowering others does not have to be a grand event. It can be helping a neighbor or someone with a job application and resume. It could be helping a co-worker analyze a project while being of support and encouragement, or it can be telling your children they can accomplish a task and giving them your vote of confidence.

EMPOWER OTHERS

Whether you are a parent, manager, employee, or teacher, most of us are going to experience leadership at some point in our lifetime, even if it is not in the formal sense. The thought of taking charge of a group of people, including our peers, can be a stressful idea. However, when focused on empowering those you lead by providing encouragement, and the necessary tools to succeed, you can empower others. According to Bill Gates, "Leaders are those who empower others."

When leading in your home, organizing a community service group, or completing a team project, create opportunities for everyone to have shared ownership. Creating ownership provides an opportunity for everyone to be involved, take control, and provide creative input.

EMPOWER OTHERS

Always give credit where it is due, and the outcome is usually a positive experience for all involved in the work.

I recall working with a group of college students who were mentoring middle school students and wanted to make a greater impact. These college students were ambitious interns working in my department and had great ideas. About halfway through their internships, they shared they did not feel they were making a difference. As a result, they wanted to do more and asked to take on a larger project. As opposed to sticking to the status quo, I allowed them to take ownership of the program, to innovate and expand in a way that felt impactful to them. The outcome was the creation of a full-day middle school to college program supporting a much larger group of students. By creating opportunity for ownership as a leader to this group, I empowered them to make a much larger impact.

For individuals in leadership positions in the workplace, another way to empower those you lead is transparency about your team's end goal. Instead of telling your team what they need to do, explain the "why" of the project and purpose. If they understand the why, they will better understand how to accomplish the end goal. This may include allowing for flex time to complete projects or getting to the finished product in a way you may not have considered.

When you empower your team, your job then becomes to nurture and support their work through encouragement and securing the tools they need to succeed. Once you realize the benefits of empowering your team, you will realize there is no reason to be stressed about leadership.

REFLECTION:

1. Who do I empower in my family?
2. Who do I empower in my community?
3. How do I know when I am empowering others?

Equipped to Serve

CHALLENGE:

When you consider where you are in life today, who can you serve to empower? How will you serve to empower?

CHAPTER 2

QUALITY TIME
WITH OTHERS

QUALITY TIME WITH OTHERS - Giving others your active engagement and focused time devoted to listening and nurturing relationships.

"The greatest gift you can give someone is your time. Because when you give your time, you are giving a portion of your life that you will never get back."
– Unknown

Several years ago, I felt like a heavyweight boxer had hit me square in the face. It was around the time my daughter was seven years old. I had planned an event for eight hundred people and invited my family. It was a rare occasion to have my family attend my work events. However, on this particular day my children did not have school, so they attended this event, which my department had created for students. After it was over, my boss asked my daughter if she was going to do something fun with daddy. My daughter responded, "No, it will be me, mommy and brother

9

Equipped to Serve

because daddy always has to work." In that instance, we all laughed, but the statement hit me at my core and was life changing. I had a decision to make about the type of person I wanted to be for my daughter. At that moment, I realized that quality time was a way to serve my daughter and family. After much reflection, what surfaced is that quality time is different from quantity time. While I attended all my daughters' activities, helped her with homework, and spent time on the weekends, she wanted an uninterrupted time that was just the two of us having fun. Often, we replace quality time with quantity time.

For some of us, the idea of quality time and balancing home, work and serving others is complicated. For example, I enjoy spending quality time with my family and value serving as a team member and showing my commitment to my career. Yet, working long hours, or taking advantage of overtime never stopped the guilt of feeling like I was not spending enough time with my wife and kids. In fact, according to a Pew Research Center study, 52% of working fathers, and 60% of working mothers, shared challenges with juggling work-family balance.[4]

Your kids may also be involved in sports or other activities like mine are, making it more challenging to notch out quality time with each other, not to mention making time for any type of community projects or continuing education you are pursuing.

It has become very easy to focus on busy work, staying busy, and constantly proving our productivity in this fast-paced world. When you add in the amount of time we now spend on social media and gaming apps, the impact on our families, organizations and teams can be costly. We then tell ourselves, "if only we had spent more time," or more quality time focused on listening, understanding, and slowing down.

Whether you are an hourly employee, a fortune 100 executive, a parent, a sibling, or a friend, we can all serve others through quality time. The only cost is our time. Quality time means giving others your active engagement and focused time during which you are devoted to listening and nurturing relationships. Quality time is a great way

10

QUALITY TIME WITH OTHERS

to show loved-ones, friends, and team members you care. Some researchers argue quality time creates loyalty. This was true for me when I served as a high school principal. Too often I was always moving, always in a rush, or was speaking to team members on the run. My team felt they could not get to me to discuss their ideas, interests, and successes. Finally, our school's special programs and magnet coordinator, Coleen Sand, talked with me about taking the time to learn about my team and their needs. Humbly, I listened to her words and began to think about the idea that my team wanted quality time with me as their leader. They wanted time beyond the day-to-day work and formal observations. As a result, I learned to slow down, spend more time in their classrooms, have more one-to-one conversations, and break bread with team members. The focus on quality time showed my team that they were important and valued. A focus on quality time paid dividends as we moved our school from meeting the state academic standards to performing above state academic standards.

Quality time in the workplace, community, and at home creates trust. Giving others your time, and spending time with them, creates an opportunity to nurture positive relationships. It is difficult to trust someone you do not know. While growing our relationships at work has a direct and tangible outcome, it is just as important to do the same for family and friendships. How often have you heard a parent say, "I don't know my teenager," or a teenager say, "My parent doesn't know me."

One of the greatest examples I've experienced of serving others through quality time was during my childhood and adolescent years at home with my mother, Margaret Hart. For my mother, giving others her active engagement and focused time devoted to listening and nurturing relationships was worth more than a new home or car. Time with others was important to my mother because she did not grow up with her parents and siblings. My mother was given away at birth to Mother Merrill, a family friend who had adopted her. Mother Merrill instilled in her the importance of family, looking out for family, and

11

Equipped to Serve

family eating meals together. Mother Merrill's home was living quarters to 15 other adopted children and was a place of respite for African American families traveling during the 1950s when hotels were not available or accessible. While living with Mother Merrill, my mother was very sickly with asthma and was told she would never have children. Of course, the rest of the story is history because you are reading my book, and she birthed three more siblings besides me.

My mother's childhood experience is the primary reason she insisted we gather as a family to sit down and eat dinner every day, and as often as possible. She learned that mealtime, regardless of work titles and positions, or age of siblings, was a simple way to connect, nurture and cherish our family. Mealtime was her way of ensuring quality time was built into our daily lives. We would often invite my friends over for dinner. Lamont Pace, one of my closest high school friends, would call our home Little House on the Prairie. Little House on the Prairie was a television show in the 1970s and 80s, and within the show they highlighted the family sitting and eating together. Eating as a family was foreign to my friend because of his parents' work schedule. In a recent poll by YouGov, 62% of parents wish family dinners with their children occurred more often.[5]

My mother's service through quality time extended far beyond the walls of our home. To this day, she lives by the phrase, "If I can help somebody, my living is not in vain." Her idea of serving others involved spending time with them. With no college degree, and no corporate leadership training, she knew that the best way to serve others is to spend time listening and nurturing. Equipped to Serve is about spending time, not money, with those you love and care about. For my friends, our home was a place of care, nurturing, and spending time together.

Another example of my mother's focus on quality time was when she visited the homes of elder members living in our community. She believed visiting the elderly showed our sense of caring for those who had come before us, and those who had, themselves, spent quality time with others during their prime years. As a child, I recall going to visit the elderly, and

12

QUALITY TIME WITH OTHERS

sitting on couches with plastic coverings that stuck to my leg. I observed the importance of going into someone's home and breaking bread with them. My mother taught us how to listen to others' concerns and to not be in a rush. She provided this same level of quality time to serving in women's ministry and serving in a women's shelter for close to 15 years.

Her work with the women's shelter involved meeting regularly with women who experienced serious life challenges, but she believed in meeting people where they were. Her goal was to be there for others because everybody needs somebody. She wanted the women to know that someone who cares is always nearby, and she created a safe space for women to share their stories. In her words: "This was a faith vision to help women. In the meetings, I wanted to give them a time to share their story. They needed a space and time to talk with other women to help them come out of whatever they were dealing with."

My mother would spend quality time at the shelter every other week with one purpose in mind: to encourage them and let them know they are loved and not alone. During her 15-year tenure, she would ensure a safe space to talk and provide a good meal for the women. Often, she would share this experience with my daughter and niece and instill in them the importance of quality time to help others who are less fortunate or encounter challenging circumstances. The act of kindness is an experience my daughter and niece remember to this day. My mother taught them to see and experience the importance of showing care and doing something kind for other women and girls. This brings me to a very important point. Serving others through quality time can be passed on to the next generation and beyond. Both my niece and daughter engage in programs and projects that promote quality time because of the value instilled in them by my mother. For example, my daughter started a culture club at her school to connect students across her campus. Some days, the group of students meets for the purpose of eating lunch together to strengthen friendships.

My mother would also give others quality time through letters

13

Equipped to Serve

titled, "Letters To My Sisters." Letters To My Sisters was her way of spending time investing in those she cared about. Each letter written served as a motivator and reminder of how special each person was to my mother. The letters became a way to serve her immediate sisters, sisters-in-law, and friends she could not see regularly. Letters to My Sisters served as a form of encouragement to other women as well. The only cost was time and about 50 envelopes and stamps. Some letters traveled to Germany, Jamaica, and South Africa. On a few occasions, her letters were read to audiences in the UK during concerts led by Freddie Poole, once back-up singer to the Supremes and other artists.

When not writing or working in women's ministry, Margaret would volunteer at a local elementary school, helping students with reading and building-up their self-esteem. Through her time in the school, she worked with many students who were historically underserved because she wanted them to feel like they mattered. Each opportunity to serve was an opportunity to share quality time with students. She did not have a college degree, let alone an elementary school reading certification, but she knew the importance of spending quality time with those in need, and so, was able to impact their lives, nonetheless.

To my mother, quality time meant helping and serving others by sharing her time. Whether serving in her community, organizing sock drives and dinners, or creating a space for women to speak, spending quality time with others is how she is equipped to serve. Equipped to serve is beyond receiving a paycheck or leading a team; it becomes a way to ensure our part in making our community and world a better place within our circle of influence. We all have influence somewhere.

SERVING OTHERS THROUGH QUALITY TIME

Quality time with your children

If you are like me, long workdays and long commutes might limit the amount of time you have to spend with your children and you

might hardly see them during the week. T¹
to become more intentional about qu⁻
shown the benefit of spending time togeth⸱
a strong sense of connectedness. In fact, som⸱
spent together increases connectedness througho␣
raised two teenagers, I always appreciated the times theɣ
connect during the day when they were in school or attendi⸱

The reality is that your children are going to consume you␣
one way or another. Make the time to build them up now to avo␣
bailing them out of a situation later. Proactive parenting will help your
children become more resilient and make wiser choices. Boost your
child's self-esteem and social skills with uninterrupted time and attention. After all, our first call to service should be to our family.

Quality time with your partner

At times, our partner or spouse may feel more like a roommate if
we let that happen. And trust me, I never wanted to spend the rest of
my life with any of my roommates. Having a roommate is a short-term
experience and our paths were always moving in different directions.
My point is that when in a relationship, the honeymoon phase will
end, but you can revitalize your relationship with quality time. For
example, ordinary kindness and time together can be just as positive
as cards, flowers, and a night out. It's important to do things as simple
as making time to listen without providing answers. Our partner or
spouse is usually the person cheering us on as we work to live out the
characteristics in this book. So, they deserve our quality time as well.

Quality time with self

Your relationship with yourself counts. Unfortunately, we often ne-
glect ourselves because of long work hours, other family needs, or trying to
burn the candle at both ends. When you honor your needs, you increase

...pacity to care for your loved ones and be at your best. I commend ...r taking some time for yourself to read this book, engage in the ques-...s at the end of each chapter, and hopefully share this book with others.

Quality time with friends and family

Spending time with family and friends is a great way to improve quality of life. Some researchers believe there is a direct connection between quality time with friends and family and the quality of life you live. Spending quality time with those we cherish allows us to create lasting memories. Traveling on vacation with siblings is sure to bring laughter to your heart while receiving advice and assurance through life's challenges. One of my fondest vacation memories is when my wife and I traveled to the Grand Canyon with our children, my siblings and their children, and my parents. Although none of the grandkids wanted to see the "big hole in the ground," the loud "wows" and the marveled look on the faces of everyone from age seven to seventy were irreplaceable. The experience will be with our families forever. Our schedules should never be too demanding to spend time with family and friends. Today is a good day to create an opportunity to spend quality time with loved ones. Spending time with loved ones is one more example of giving others your active engagement and focused time devoted to listening and nurturing relationships.

> *Today is a good day to create an opportunity to spend quality time with loved ones.*

QUALITY TIME WITH OTHERS

Quality time with coworkers

When we watch the news or scroll through social media, we see many stories highlighting the idea of "them vs us." We see division in political perspectives, social beliefs, how to run our local schools, and many other areas of life. One way to strengthen our collectiveness, or what my mentor Clifton Taulbert calls "brotherhood for all mankind," is to spend quality time with co-workers. Supervisors and co-workers alike have an opportunity to create quality conversation spaces that promote uninterrupted listening and learning from each other. Furthermore, as discussions around diversity, equity, and inclusion continue gaining traction in the workplace, serving others through quality time promotes learning about each other, sharing experiences, and understanding our similarities and differences. To know me, you must spend time with me.

REFLECTION:

- What can I do to serve others through quality time?
- How can I apply quality time in my work as a leader or team member?
- Who do I need to serve through quality time? What will be my commitment?
- What does quality time really look like for my family?

CHAPTER 3

UNSELFISHNESS TOWARDS OTHERS

UNSELFISHNESS TOWARDS OTHERS - The quality of putting another person first and a willingness to give of your time, money, and resources for the good of others.

> "The unselfish effort to bring cheer to others will be the beginning of a happier life for ourselves."
> –Helen Keller

Like the principles discussed in the prior chapters, unselfishness requires an action toward others. Unselfishness towards others is a form of service that can be very simple or extremely complex. Unselfishness can be as simple as allowing someone to go ahead of you in line. However, it can become more complex when examining the idea of putting someone else's needs before your needs. The idea of unselfishness is by no means a new topic, and has been explored by educators, religious leaders, and scholars around the world. According to many, unselfishness is the path to happiness. Helen Keller, once advocate for disability rights, was quoted as saying, "The unselfish effort to bring cheer to others will be the beginning of a happier life for ourselves." Like Helen Keller, I agree there is a sense of happiness when we show unselfishness towards others. When we exhibit unselfishness, we build community because we show care and interest in those around us and foster goodwill among a group. Being unselfish allows us to decenter ourselves, and view clearly the views, needs, and hopes of the collective. Clifton L. Taulbert, author, speaker, and mentor stated it this way: "Unselfishness is the currency that drives community." Unselfishness towards each other strengthens our sense of belonging and community.

> **"Unselfishness is the currency that drives community."**
> – Clifton L. Taulbert

Yet, in society, we are often taught directly and indirectly that finishing first is best and focusing on the self is best. We spend a lot of time centered on winning and being the best. We grow up hearing phrases like "nice gals/guys finish last," or "the early bird gets the worm." We are taught to concentrate on our own goals, dreams, and aspirations. At a young age, we are inundated with the benefits of winning and having the bragging rights to say, "I won first place." In the sports world, we see young athletes coached by parents who want their child to be the star, regardless of other talent on the team that might be better. At the same time, you may see parents who argue with coaches because their child is not the star. At the end of the day, an expectation is created that "it is all about me." Winning, finishing first, and being

Equipped to Serve

the best is something we strive for as adults, and something we want for our children. However, the act of unselfishness goes beyond our individual selves and puts us in a position to be equipped to serve others. If a child were to learn, say, the value of working together as a team to solve problems, they would be able to both help bring their team to victory while also making friendships, and learning to collaborate with and care for others – a skill that will be valued for a lifetime. Show me a championship team and I will show you unselfishness in practice.

We witnessed selfishness on an international level during the COVID-19 Pandemic that began in 2020. In the United States, something as simple as wearing a mouth and nose covering to protect each other from spreading a deadly virus was front and center in political debates. Around the world, in less than two years during 2020 and 2021, more than 5-million people had died due to the COVID-19 virus. In the US, 1,000,000 people died of COVID-19 and the debate over wearing a mask landed in multiple state and federal courts. Although much national and international research proved the benefits of wearing a mask/face-covering to protect from spreading the deadly disease, some people felt it was their personal right to not wear a mask, regardless of the potential harm to self or others. However, in an era where selfishness was visibly experienced from our local communities to the national and international community, unselfishness is manifest all around us. During this same pandemic, hundreds of thousands of service providers, from food servers and custodians to medical workers and first responders, put their lives on the line for the health and safety of the US and world. While some considered only their personal freedom and the slight discomfort of a mask on their face, others channeled their energy into serving their community during a time of need.

Unselfishness is the quality of putting another person's needs first and a willingness to share your time, money, and resources for the good of others. The act of unselfishness reminds me of a quote my college professor and one-time business partner, Ron Keys, would always say

20

UNSELFISHNESS TOWARDS OTHERS

when an opportunity arose to help someone. He would share, "the power in receiving is giving." He was referring to the idea that unselfishness always has a positive benefit to the giver.

During my time on earth, I have been the beneficiary of unselfishness on many occasions. In fact, we all have at some point. One encounter I recall a few years ago was when my wife called while I was at work. She shared a snake was in our backyard and was afraid because it had reached our back porch. At the time, I was at work, and it would take me 45 minutes to get home. Realizing I would not get home fast enough to deal with the situation, I called my neighbor Will Hess, a retired police officer, to help. Will and I don't hang out, we talk mostly in passing about our children, and we have different political views and cultural experiences. However, he immediately stopped what he was doing and walked across the street to my home to assist my wife. He had no clue how large and dangerous the snake would be, but he unselfishly responded to our need. Gratefully, Will found the snake and removed it from our yard. I'm sure many of you can think of examples where someone in your life exemplified the quality of putting another person first.

Whether you grew up with caring parents who put your daily needs before theirs, or you grew up with a friend who was always kind to you, most of us have lived on the receiving end of unselfishness. Even if you did not grow up with caring parents, someone had to care for you from infancy into your teenage years. Some of you reading are parents, and some of you may be parent to a child you did not bring into this world. For me, raising another person's child is a great example of unselfishness. Parenting in general is one of the ultimate examples of unselfishness. One of the greatest compliments my biological father (JD Hill) gave my dad (my father who raised me) was when he told my dad, "You did what I could not do." He gave my dad credit for raising me from infancy to manhood even though it's difficult and complicated for most to admit this. However, the story doesn't end there.

21

Equipped to Serve

My birth father shared his comment during a keynote speech with approximately 500 other people watching and listening. His compliment to my dad was unselfish to begin with, but it was even more so to share it with a large group as opposed to one-on-one with no one else around. Instead, he put his shortcoming out in front of 500 other people, humbled himself, and gave credit to my dad. The unselfish act caused a chain reaction of gratitude in the room and a sense of hope for many who had lived a similar circumstance.

As I grow more mature in age, it seems as though each prior generation comments on the selfishness and self-absorbedness of the next generation. On many occasions, I can recall being told "your generation is selfish." I can also recall conversations with peers or listening in on conversations of others discussing what they perceive to be an increase in selfishness or self-centeredness. However, I would like to share a different perspective on the idea of unselfishness. I believe that all of us as humans have a greater percent or level of unselfishness than selfishness residing in each of us, and we need only cultivate what is already there. Despite this, I believe our society and media give greater attention to the massive amounts of selfish acts playing out in our world daily. All we must do is watch the news each day, stop by the water cooler at work, or listen to screaming parents at sporting events. Generally, what comes to mind is peoples' encounters with other people resulting in some form of negative selfish act. Whether it's a parent yelling for their child to be put in the game because they believe their child should be the star, a reality TV show where individuals purposefully focus on selfish interests to stay on the show, or the overwhelming constant negative news showing fallout between various parties for not getting what they want, the concept of selfishness is promoted and perpetuated. The showcasing of negativity confirms what our minds are already conditioned to believe: that selfishness is abound in our world.

Although selfishness abounds, I believe at the core of all of us is a need for community. We have a need to be part of something, a

22

UNSELFISHNESS TOWARDS OTHERS

need for relationship with family, friends, co-workers, and the community we live and serve in. According to Clifton Taulbert, creator of The Building Community Institute, "Unselfishness is the currency that drives community." I believe it is the same currency that motivated Mother Teresa and Martin L. King, Jr. to unselfishly serve the greater society. It is the same currency that drove my parents to serve, and it is the same currency that drives many of us to willingly give our time, money, and resources for the good of others.

Take, for example, the life stories of Fred and Tiffany Lux. I encountered the Lux's when my children where in elementary school. My wife and I wanted to increase our children's physical activity and were informed to try club track by a friend. My friend shared the experience would help our children with other sports throughout the year, so we reached out to Fred Lux. During our first meeting, I learned Fred worked as a repair person doing odd jobs and landscape work, and Tiffany worked in childcare. Amazingly, the Lux's have led a club track team for close to 30 years, spanning multiple generations. In fact, they have coached the grandchildren of some of their very first athletes. Their club team supports athletes ages four to eighteen, and at times they are serving close to 100 athletes. Each year, the Lux's, along with their coaching staff, take 10-30 athletes to the state, regional and USA National Junior Olympics. Some of their athletes have set state records, became national junior Olympians and All-Americans, and have represented their local schools at city and state championships. Many of their rising athletes have gone on to become college student athletes in various sports, and some have gone on to pursue professional athletic careers that include the National Football League.

When reading the short and dynamic history of the Lux Family, and if you know anything about club sports, it may seem as though they were able to create a very successful cash cow to support their love of track and field. However, that is far from the truth and what makes them a perfect example of unselfishness. At the forefront is a couple

23

Equipped to Serve

committed to putting other people first and willingly giving their time, money, and resources for the good of others. Most of the youth and families they serve come from lower-income families and single-mother families. To include as many athletes as possible, the Lux's keep fees low and offer scholarship support to many of the young athletes which results in free travel, paid competition fees, free track shoes, and at times, meals, and transportation to and from practice. Someone once shared that Fred would give the shirt off his back to a student in need. I saw this first-hand for athletes not able to purchase the needed track shoes for competition. The Lux's started their track club with a $1,000 investment. That investment has positively impacted over 1,000 youth and their parents, and it continues. Both Fred and Tiffany found a way to serve others through building a positive community that allows belonging and success for young athletes and reverberates into the wider community. Equipped to serve is about identifying how each of us as individuals can serve others, regardless of the titles we have or don't have, and regardless of the income we have or don't have. We all have something special to offer in our service to others and only need to search within ourselves to find it.

I asked Fred and Tiffany why they chose a track club as their way to serve others through unselfishness. Below is what I learned:

Fred: "We wanted to make a difference in the kids' lives in our community. We didn't have that opportunity growing up, so we wanted to do something positive. It started as an outreach to keep kids off streets; it started with football – nothing for the kids to do – everything for the kids to do nowadays costs money; costs that many single parents don't have. When I was a kid, we had free parks and recreation, and free afterschool programs. Nowadays everything costs money."

Tiffany: "We began to reach out to help as many as we can. Helping single moms with something positive for their children. We've been doing this for over 25 years and have had 100 athletes at times."

Fred: "I grew up in Tucson, AZ. I wanted to see kids have an

UNSELFISHNESS TOWARDS OTHERS

opportunity, and I wanted to be a positive role model. I wanted to see kids make it to the next level and let them know that track can help open other doors for them, including their other sports, to go to college. I wanted to show the kids in my neighborhood that they could go further than high school. Growing up, I was fortunate to have a dad. My dad was my coach, and he would play all types of ball with me and my cousins. I got pretty good at football and ended up playing for a small college. Unfortunately, my dad got sick, and I couldn't focus on playing. I had a rough time with the coaches and did not have anyone to lead me. The head football coach didn't know I could play or that I had talent until he put me in the game. I exceled on the field during the season but missed an exam to go home and see my dad who was sick. My coach told me not to come back. So, I stayed home, and my dad passed away from a brain tumor. I didn't have anyone to push me. After leaving school, my teammate told me several NFL scouts showed up, but I was gone – it was too late for me. That is when I decided I can help youth make better decisions so that they can go further in life. I grew up on the southside of town in a poor area. Most people in my community didn't go far in life. They wanted a job, wanted to have fun and drink. My dream was to go to the NFL. So now when I am not working, I help as many athletes as possible to achieve their goals."

Tiffany: "I grew up playing sports. I ran track and played basketball. When I started high school, I already had one basketball scholarship offer. In my junior and senior year of high school I made the all-city and all-state teams and was selected as an All American. In one basketball game I had 28 rebounds and tied for second in the state conference record books. I wanted to play basketball in college, but my coach didn't give me my college letters. I was under age eighteen my senior year, and I could not talk to college coaches. I received letters from colleges two years after graduation, but by then I decided to get married, I was pregnant and had started a family. My experience causes me to advocate for other young mothers and their athletes. When you

Equipped to Serve

grow up you don't want to be a product of a negative environment or experience. So, we wanted to make a change in our community."

Learning of the Lux's life experiences and why they choose to serve unselfishly in this way is one example that we can all learn from. They don't brag, they don't look for the big money, they don't look for reward. Tiffany shared, when asked about success, "Our payoff is seeing the kids succeed in high school and college. We like seeing the expressions on the parents faces from when their child finishes a race for the first time to seeing their child compete at nationals, something they had not ever considered before joining our club. We also get excited every time a new club starts from our club. Now there are three or four clubs across Arizona and California."

For close to 30 years, the Lux's have unselfishly put others first and willingly gave their time, money, and resources for the good of others. Imagine coaching a track club without pay three to five times per week for 7 months, plus all-day track meets at least 14 times per year, and traveling to each meet 120 to 1,300 miles away, for 30 years.

The impact of their track club lasts far beyond just young athletes becoming successful in sports. Take, for example, Levi Wallace, a professional athlete who once ran track for Fred Lux. Over the course of several years Levi donated and gave back to the city and community he grew up in to help hundreds of families with food insecurities and support during the holidays. More amazing is that he gave his personal cell phone number to anyone wanting to talk or needing a voice to listen during the peak of an international pandemic in 2020. In his words, "Everyone's going through the same thing that I am, sitting at home. I just thought that people need to be encouraged." Levi would end up receiving about 500 calls, and he returned every call.

Like the Lux family, there are many more examples and stories of everyday people living and serving unselfishly. From the people who put their lives at stake during natural and unnatural disasters serving as volunteer firefighters, to the millions of people who give their time and

26

UNSELFISHNESS TOWARDS OTHERS

money year in and year out, serving others through unselfish acts is a part of our DNA. We see unselfishness lived out when a mother generously cares for her family by putting her needs last, or when a father makes sacrifices for the betterment of his children, or educators who spend a portion of their paycheck every month to ensure their students have what they need including supplies for their classrooms, motivation, and prizes. We all have the ability to serve others. We are equipped to serve through unselfishness, whether it be small acts of random kindness or larger projects like the Lux family's track club. I am fortunate because I get to witness unselfishness daily. For example, witnessing a team member share small gifts with students who improve in their academic achievement, a coordinator who says, "I'm treating you to lunch today," my children offering to extend a helping hand when I am working on a project, or for years watching my wife make kind bracelets and give "kind bars" to the ladies in her civic group. Each of these acts were based on putting another person first and a willingness to give their time, money, and resources for the good of others.

At the beginning of this chapter, I mentioned how I believe we all have more unselfishness in us than selfishness, and that we see way too much of the selfish side of humans in the media and news. For example, human nature seems to enjoy seeing stories about famous people making big mistakes in selfish ways; what if we spent more time learning about the unselfish acts of these same individuals. It may change our outlook on life. Take, for example professional athletes and entertainers. Many donate to charitable causes year-round though we may never hear about it. Though if they make a mistake or say something that is less than savory, it is plastered over every news source for the world to see. As I've stated before, equipped to serve is about putting another person first and a willingness to give your time, money, and resources for the good of others. We all can serve through our time, money, and resources, and make an effort to see the unselfishness of others, even when it's hard to find.

Equipped to Serve

EVERYDAY UNSELFISH ACTS

When my son was in third grade, an older student that he did not know called my son the N-word, a racial slur which I will not spell out here in full. It was the first time my son would be called the N-word, causing him to go into a shocked and frozen state. When the incident happened, a young man named Sean stood up for my son and stopped the other student from bullying. Sean could have kept to himself, but instead he acted unselfishly to help a younger student. For my son, he recognized that hatred existed. However, more importantly, he experienced an example of unselfishness and social justice on the micro level. Since that experience in third grade, my son has had his share of standing up for classmates and teammates and promoting a better world to live in himself.

Every year, my mother solicits help from me, my siblings, and our families to do a sock drive to support those in need. Another example is when my good friend Wesley Dawson leads a corporate office team in hosting a veterans' 5K run to raise money for veterans, or the nurses in a hospital taking time to celebrate the recovery and release of a patient healthy enough to return to their own home.

Additional examples include a church ministry founded to reduce hunger, homelessness, and suffering in their community with the help of other volunteer organizations in their community. It may be opening a door for someone, helping a senior citizen put their groceries in their car, grabbing something off the top shelf in a store if you are tall enough, not taking advantage of a cashier who gives you more money than required, ensuring a good tip for your waiter who took care of you at a restaurant. Or maybe it's simply saying thank you.

REFLECTION:

1. In what ways do I extend unselfishness towards others around me?

UNSELFISHNESS TOWARDS OTHERS

2. In what other ways do I practice unselfishness towards my friends, and co-workers?

3. How do I model unselfishness for my loved ones (spouse/significant other/children/siblings/parents)?

CHALLENGE:

Commit to registering or signing-up with a local volunteer organization in the next 10 days. If you are volunteering with an organization, consider taking on a greater role within the next 30 days. In either case, consider partnering with a family member or friend to volunteer.

CHAPTER 4

INSPIRE OTHERS

INSPIRE OTHERS - Giving others the motivation to be their best and achieve a goal because of your actions and or words.

> "If your actions inspire others to dream more, learn more, do more, and become more, you are a leader." –John Quincy Adams

At times, life can be difficult, and the idea of reaching the pot of gold at the end of the rainbow can seem next to impossible. However, we have the ability to find inspiration in nature, people, and events happening all around us. Unfortunately, at the same time, in today's fast-paced environment, where social media, memes, and a desire for overnight success have become an obsession, people who inspire others are needed more than ever before. According to Scott Kaufman, psychology professor, "Inspiration propels a person from apathy to possibility, and transforms the way we perceive our own capabilities."[6] Dr. Kaufman argues that inspiration can be activated, captured, and manipulated to impact life outcomes. Examples throughout history highlight the lasting impact that people who inspire others have on our global society.

INSPIRE OTHERS

Through a passion or purpose, such individuals motivate others to be their best and provide inspiration for people to reach beyond what they believed could be. Venus and Serena Williams inspired a generation of US Open and Wimbledon hopefuls. Jessica Cox, armless at birth and an airplane pilot, motivates people to look beyond their own limiting beliefs. Tiger Woods made golf as popular as Oprah Winfrey and Michael Jordan. Walt Disney, creator of Disneyland, reminded us to use our imagination and dream big.

Then there are those who inspired generations and countries through their sacrifice and courage. Rosa Parks, a seamstress living in Montgomery, Alabama, refused to give up her seat on a segregated bus in 1955. Her actions inspired a movement that would ultimately end segregation in the United States. Mrs. Parks did not allow circumstances or status quo practices to stop her from serving as an inspiration to others.

Like Rosa Parks, Malala Yousafzai did not allow her circumstance or status quo practices to stop her from serving as an inspiration to others. Engaged in activism at the age of 11 years old, she campaigned for girls to have a right to attend school in her home country. At age 15, she was shot by a Taliban soldier in her homeland of Pakistan, and at age 17, she won the Nobel Peace Prize for her continued advocacy for girls worldwide to receive a free education.

To inspire others is to serve others. Sometimes we can inspire others based on our attitude about life. Nick Vujicic, an international motivational speaker, often says, "Change your attitude, change your life." Mr. Vujicic is another example of not allowing circumstances or status quo practices to stop one from serving as an inspiration to others. Born with no arms or legs, Nick uses his life experiences to motivate and inspire others worldwide. He is considered one of most inspiration people of the 21st Century.

Those who inspire others are all around us if we look close enough. I find inspiration in my family, in my spouse whose story is

Equipped to Serve

highlighted later in this book. I find inspiration in my children – my daughter for her blunt honesty and desire to make the world a better place using her voice and activism, and my son who has overcome several obstacles and has persisted to play sports at the highest level in college while fighting for equity and fairness for others. The key to inspiring others is to share your story without shame because your story can inspire others. To receive inspiration is a good thing. To give inspiration is a great thing.

My mentor, who I've mentioned, Clifton Taulbert is an international best-selling author who serves as an inspiration to me and thousands of others around the globe. His book, Eight Habits of the Heart has inspired me to focus on striving daily to be the best version of myself, reach a benchmark, and continue improving. His actions have inspired me to be more. Our sixth US President, John Quincy Adams, wrote, "If your actions inspire others to dream more, learn more, do more and become more, you are a leader."

Someone who lives out "inspiring others" is a young, distinguished gentleman named Trehon Cockrell-Coleman. Trehon serves as an inspirational leader who inspires others to dream more, learn more, do more, and become more. I first met Mr. Coleman during a Sunday church service where I was given the opportunity to speak about my work. Years later, my family and I would become members of the same church as Mr. Coleman. Our first interaction, and Trehon's ability to inspire my son, who had traveled with me, would leave a lasting impression that would come full circle.

When I began writing this chapter on inspiration, he was the image that came to the forefront of my thought process. At first glance, you see a young man that grew up in a home with strict parents who prepared him to navigate the world, someone who benefited from others sowing seeds of inspiration in his life. In Trehon's words:

Much of who I am is rooted in my upbringing and raising. As much as I felt like I lived under strict rules as a child, my parents' very

INSPIRE OTHERS

structure unquestionably prepared me to navigate places and spaces well beyond my age and across generations. As I learned to navigate the spaces, I was the beneficiary of people seeing a small glimpse of themselves in me and would sow into my life. Each interaction provided opportunities for me to make decisions that would constantly mold and shape my destiny regardless of where I was at in life. Therefore, I work to inspire others.

Mr. Coleman's comments read like a life-story planned for success at birth. However, we know there is always more to the story in life.

Mr. Coleman would later share how he had to overcome the obstacle of not growing up with his biological mother and all that is associated with not living with the person that gave birth to you. Not having his mother deeply impacted his self-esteem. In elementary school, he was put in speech classes due to being diagnosed with a speech impediment, and at another point in life, he was ashamed to smile because of his overbite. When all his friends were planning for scholarships and college enrollment during their senior year in high school, Trehon feared telling anyone he achieved a 14 on the ACT and was required to take remedial classes his first year of college. When he got to college, the years of feeling like he was less than or the idea that he did not grow up with his mother would bother him.

Like Trehon, many of us have felt abandoned, neglected, unworthy, or unprepared, which is why his story of inspiration is important. Through his challenges and feelings of shortcoming, he realized that his circumstances, and his ability to overcome his circumstances, could inspire both young and mature. Instead of focusing on what he did not have, he remembered that he was the beneficiary of people seeing something positive in him and would sow positive seeds into his life. Trehon used inspiration from others to become an inspiration. Equipped to serve is about taking the best of what you have, and the obstacles you have conquered to inspire others to be better.

Equipped to Serve

Fast forward to the present, Trehon is a thriving millennial who inspires others. He conquered his elementary, high school and college challenges to complete his bachelor's and master's degree. He defeated his speech impediment and fear of smiling to become a dynamic speaker to crowds young and mature, in-person and virtually. Furthermore, he explains, "I am grateful for the gift of sharing and speaking my story of becoming so that it can live in the hearts of others as they reflect on being equipped to serve." Trehon has taken on the moral obligation to serve others through inspiration. For many years, he volunteered as a youth pastor leading what I would consider one of the most progressive youth ministries in the state of Arizona. His inspiring leadership, dynamic team, and collaboration with families has produced youth activists, scholars, artists, creators, and top athletes around the country.

To inspire is not about position, money, or status, but about giving others the motivation to be their best and achieve a goal because of your actions and or words. According to the late, great Ella Fitzgerald, "Where there is love and inspiration, I don't think you can go wrong." Like Ella Fitzgerald, I believe we can't lose when there is love and inspiration. Equipped serve is about giving others the motivation to be their best and achieve a goal because of your actions and or words. Serving as an inspirer unselfishly looks beyond your own circumstances and uses your lived experiences to share how you overcame obstacles to inspire others.

WAYS TO INSPIRE OTHERS

Inspiring others does not have to be a grand event, result in a national championship, or highlight an obstacle someone conquered on national television. Like Trehon, inspiring others may come in the form of volunteering and unselfish acts of kindness, or simply sharing your own story of overcoming obstacles. Someone may be inspired by

INSPIRE OTHERS

the way you handle yourself in tough situations, or how you endure through a crisis. For others, rather than sharing your own story, they may need you to serve as a listening ear to lead them toward their own ideas and inspiration. Inspiration may come in the form of helping someone find a spark of excitement for their future.

On the job, inspiring others may show-up in the form of listening to a co-worker's innovative ideas or opinions about a different way to complete a task or implement a program. Serving as an inspiration may involve helping a loved one see the hidden beauty in everyday experiences and surroundings.

Even a trip to the local museum or a national park in your home state can serve as an inspiration. As I shared in chapter two, I am reminded of the time I took my children to the Grand Canyon. The Grand Canyon is about a four-hour drive from my home. Prior to seeing the Canyon, both of my children (age 16 and 20) wanted to take a different vacation or just stay home. After all, it was just a big hole in the ground. Upon making the four-hour drive, and the short walk to our first view of the south rim, they both were blown away by the beauty and massiveness of this great natural masterpiece. Both my children were inspired because they had not experienced the massive natural beauty of the Grand Canyon before. The inspiration did not come from a social media post or the latest gadget, instead it was inspired by nature. Like the quote by Laura Ingalls Wilder, "Some old-fashioned things like fresh air and sunshine are hard to beat." Equipped to serve is about inspiring others, and it does not always have to cost a lot of money; it can simply be providing and encouraging access to inspiring places and experiences.

You never know how your own knowledge and experiences may inspire a person. For example, a motivational quote or an affirmation to a relative or friend can generate inspiration. Jesse Jackson, civil rights leader, inspired people throughout the US when he reminded individuals to say, "I am somebody." "I am somebody" is a reminder that

Equipped to Serve

we can all inspire and can all be inspired.

There are many ways to inspire others: share inspirational quotes, have the courage to share your own life story, visit a free museum, take time to listen to your neighbor's life experiences, lead with your own inspiring actions, share movies and online video clips about inspiration, and a host of other ideas. Equipped to serve is not about spending large sums of money to motivate people. Equipped to serve is about inspiring others through your actions, a kind spirit, and a nurturing attitude. Taulbert explains, "a nurturing attitude is characterized by unselfish caring, supportiveness, and a willingness to share time." Time shared can create inspiration for our family, friends, and co-workers.

HOW LEADERS CAN INSPIRE OTHERS

We all have the ability to lead and will likely lead at some point in our life. Whether we are leading a team of staff for a company, working in a supervisory role, serving as a pastor, or leading in our home, we all can inspire others. However, there is a difference between being a boss, or someone in charge, and being an inspiring leader. Inspiring leaders are those who motivate their teams, congregations, and families to accomplish and achieve goals beyond what was believed possible. Leaders who inspire take the time to learn the strengths and challenges of those they serve, and empower their teams to grow in their work, glow in their work, and go to new heights and opportunities.

Other ways to fuel inspiration in those you serve are through opportunities to make their communities and world a better place. For example, promote volunteering on a charitable board, a company network, or a local public-school board. Equipped to serve is about motivating and inspiring others to be their best.

36

INSPIRE OTHERS

REFLECTION:

1. Who inspires me and why?
2. Which of my characteristics might inspire others?
3. How can I inspire others through my actions and words?
4. What keeps me going on the days I feel uninspired?

CHALLENGE:

Who can I be an inspiration to or for? What can I do to inspire them?

CHAPTER 5

POSITIVE ATTITUDE TOWARDS OTHERS

POSITIVE ATTITUDE – a mindset that sees the good in people, groups, and situations regardless of favorable or unfavorable outcomes.
   "Positive thinking is powerful!"

Growing up, you may have heard a parent, mentor, or educator quote, "It is your attitude that determines your altitude." You might have heard a more lengthy but similar statement from the late great motivational speaker, Zig Zigler, "It is your attitude, more than your aptitude, that will determine your altitude." Regardless of which version of the statement you've heard, the bottom line is that we have a choice in how we respond to people, circumstances, and situations.

According to a Mayo Clinic article, an attitude of positive thinking can help with stress management and can improve your health.[7] Positive thoughts produce positive outcomes. When we approach all aspects of our life with positivity, we create a sense of self-empowerment that helps to pushout negative actions, thoughts, and outcomes. In fact, some researchers speculate that a positive attitude may reduce

POSITIVE ATTITUDE TOWARDS OTHERS

depression, reduce stress, strengthen your immune system, and improve a person's overall well-being.

To be clear, having a positive attitude is different than portraying "toxic positivity." Toxic positivity argues no matter how awful a situation is, people should remain 100% positive. An example might be if you tell a friend something you are struggling with, and they respond by saying "you should be thankful – others have it so much worse!" Personally, a few years ago, my family and I took a whale watching trip into the Gulf of Alaska and during the boat ride I got very sick. The boat staff commended me on how well I was doing even though I seemed to get worse with every compliment. Nothing positive came of this situation until I finally got back to land and was able to sit still. The staff used false reassurances to convince me I was doing well which was farthest from the truth. In this situation, their positivity was actually toxic for me because I felt they weren't acknowledging my distress and were dismissing my emotions. So, when I discuss positive attitude, that positivity should come from a place of truthfulness and compassion, and not empty acts to make oneself feel better.

I believe we were born into this world with a positive attitude. If you don't believe me, think about every child under the age of one and their optimism to walk. Regardless of how many times a 10-month-old child will fall, after standing up, they continue to try, and eventually they succeed. Once they stand, they try to walk. They may only make it two to five steps before falling flat on their butt. However, they get back up and keep trying until they succeed at five steps, then 10 steps and so on.

Years ago, during my career serving as a school principal, I had the privilege of running into Jon Gordon, a thought leader on positivity. We happened to be on the elevator together on our way to the same banquet hall where Jon would serve as the keynote speaker. I remember Mr. Gordon speaking about his concept called energy bus and the idea of powering your bus with positive energy. The point was to reduce the

39

Equipped to Serve

negative influences around you. Jon used the concept of an energy bus to get rid of negative folks and build a positive supportive community. He asked us to envision our minds as a bus, and each person that sits on that bus is a positive or negative influence. You are the conductor of your bus and get to choose who enters and who is not admitted. In other words, you can make the choice to fill your energy bus with positivity. We all would much rather travel through life and our careers surrounded by people who believe in our work and our ability to be a success.

Over the years, I have followed Mr. Gordon's work and appreciate this quote: "We are positive, not because life is easy. We are positive because life can be hard." Like Jon, I believe it is important for us to keep a positive outlook on life and find ways to move forward.

As I continue to mature through life, I have been blessed to encounter many people with a positive attitude. Some folks I encountered over the years at work, like Ms. Diane my first office manager when I served as a school principal, or Dr. Lupita Garcia and Jim Fish, past supervisors. Others I encountered as I matriculated through life, like my mentor Clifton L. Taulbert, my Pops J.D. Hill and Sis. Pennywell from the church I attend. Sis. Pennywell, born during the silent generation years, doesn't look a day over 60. There is a lot to be said about the benefits of a positive attitude. Each of the individuals I mention above shared a mindset that saw the good in people and saw the good in me. They lived out what it means to see good in people, groups, and situations regardless of favorable or unfavorable outcomes. Because of their ability to see the good in me, I came to see it, too, and was able to become my truest and most successful self. I took this as a lesson to see the positive in others in my own life, offering the same perspective that I was given.

At age 36, I was fortunate to work with one of the most positive people I've ever known. Sabrina Mejia served as our school attendance

40

POSITIVE ATTITUDE TOWARDS OTHERS

clerk during my years as a high school principal in Arizona. Sabrina always smiled and greeted everyone with positive energy regardless of the circumstance. I would joke with her that the sky could be falling, an earthquake just hit our region, and a tornado is coming down the street, and she would be the person to say, "It is okay, we can figure this out, and how may I help you." Her positivity was very contagious and ensured that no matter what or how the students, parents, and staff were feeling, by the time they left her desk, they were calm and at peace because their voice was heard, and they knew that help would be provided. Each morning, Sabrina, and my office manager Diane would have an office full of students. Our sitting area in the office was small, maybe enough for three people to sit, and plenty of seating outside of our main office. However, sometimes 5 to 6 students in different waves would come in not because they were required, but because they wanted to feel valued. The students wanted to know that their day would be okay, and they wanted to hear something positive. And without stating the obvious, Sabrina would smile. It was just the right amount of positivity and hope they needed to get through the day.

One day I asked Sabrina, "Why are you always so positive?" This is what she shared:

"As the youngest of four siblings, I was raised in a home with two loving protective parents. Growing up with my parents, the foundation of my upbringing was to always find the good in any circumstance. This is important since I have faced many difficulties and challenges. A strong family foundation, surrounded by supportive loved ones and a strong faith influenced my outlook on life. I have learned practical ways of applying the principles found in the Scriptures to everyday life and with my interactions with others.

Life is full of lessons, and life will test us in many ways. We have no control over the actions of others, but our own. I choose to be happy and to control or limit the negative effects any situation could have on me. As a result, I have learned that being positive is more than

41

just a state of mind, it is a way of life. In my opinion, positivity is the result of being kind, compassionate, a good listener, non-judgmental and overall showing genuine interest in others. That is what I strive to be. I strongly believe that you treat others the way you would like to be treated.

A smile, a greeting, a simple gesture, empathy towards others are powerful tools, and sometimes all that may be required to brighten up someone's day. When your happiness and joy are genuine, you can't help but be happy and, in turn can have a significant impact on those around you. I try to model this for our students and parents because many are working through challenges, disappointments, and obstacles."

Although Sabrina's work is in the public school environment, our schools are a microcosm of society. We have many hurting people, whether they are struggling financially, working through a family situation, struggling with past trauma, or having financial success, and all seems good, we all need to be in the presence of positive people. Even negative folk need positive people to help them through their hurt, pain, and struggle for inner peace. Like my students, our society can gain from having more positive people in the world. Not the type of positivity that comes with winning a prize, or getting a pay raise, or a gift you were hoping for, but the type of positive attitude that believes today is a blessing, and each breath we take is a blessing. We saw this playout in real time in the media and on social media, more times than we would like to remember, when watching nurses and hospital staff around the country celebrate the recovery of COVID-19 patients as they left the hospital during the height of the pandemic. Those fortunate to recover received a small but significant message from the hand claps and congratulations, a message of positivity that can only come from those who serve others.

Exhibiting a positive attitude toward others who are not like you, or those who have different interests, may serve to help people in your network see a different perspective. Having a positive attitude towards

POSITIVE ATTITUDE TOWARDS OTHERS

others can break-through stereotypes and biases. When you think positively about who a person is as an individual, you are less likely to allow negative stereotypes, whether true or perceived, to get in the way of building a trusting relationship. You are less likely to be influenced by what you've heard about a person, or others like them. In turn, you get to set the temperature for how you connect with others and build positive relationships. My Pastor, Amos Lewis, would share, "you have a choice to be the thermostat in a room and not the thermometer." Thermometers can only read the temperature in a room; it fluctuates based on other variables. However, a thermostat controls the temperature and has an impact on all who enter the room. One person's positive energy can act as a thermostat, cleansing the energy and uplifting a whole room.

> # "You have a choice to be the thermostat in a room and not the thermometer."
> – Amos L. Lewis

Living as a positive thermostat means you get to decide how positive you will be when walking in a room and interacting with others. As a thermostat, you get to control the outcome. Unfortunately, for those individuals who choose to be a thermometer, they can only read the temperature as it adjusts and, in short, constantly change based on others' feelings or opinions. They don't believe they have the choice to be positive. Negative people may come around to break your positive spirit, but you just keep spreading positive energy.

We encounter negative people all around us daily. You don't have

43

Equipped to Serve

to look very far to find someone that has a negative outlook on life. However, you don't have to allow destructive people to drag you down with them, either. In fact, you might be able to save a few of them, or at least make them smile for a change. They might even thank you for it. Negative people can sometimes benefit from having their perspective shaken up a little. You can be the person that causes them to question their negative way of life. Consider it to be charitable work that doesn't burden your schedule or your bank account.

When we are positive, we apply the Law of Attraction to connect with other positive people. The Law of Attraction states positivity attracts positivity, and negativity attracts negativity. The idea is that if we focus on the positive, we'll be rewarded with positive outcomes. In contrast, the obvious would be if you focus on all the negative things in your life, you'll attract other negative outcomes. According to the late Henry Ford, creator of Ford Motor Company, "Whether you think you can or think you can't, either way, you are right."

Throughout history, there are many examples and documented cases of people achieving amazing, and at times what many believe to be impossible, results by having a mindset of positive thinking. From athletes, to inventors, US Presidents, TV Personalities, and everyday people, having a positive attitude was the difference-maker in overcoming an obstacle. Take, for example, Shaquem Griffin. Griffin, a pro football player, drafted by the Seattle Seahawks in 2018, did what no other athlete had done in the history of college football or the National Football League (NFL). Griffin played at the highest level in college, was named the American Athletic Conference Defensive Player of the Year and was drafted in the fifth round of the NFL draft having only one hand.[8] According to his biography, he was born with amniotic band syndrome that would ultimately require his left hand to be amputated at the age of four.[9]

His positive attitude in overcoming what seemed impossible would spark a nation of youth with congenital disabilities to believe they could

POSITIVE ATTITUDE TOWARDS OTHERS

achieve anything and was highlighted in the Gillette (razor company) commercial titled "Shaquem Griffin: Your Best Never Comes Easy." Griffin's story exemplifies the idea that a positive attitude is a mindset that sees the good in people, groups, and situations regardless of favorable or unfavorable outcomes.

More importantly, if we dig deeper, each person who overcame a major obstacle or accomplished a great achievement had a positive person motivating them behind the scenes. Equipped to Seve is about having a mindset that sees the good in people, groups, and situations regardless of favorable or unfavorable outcomes. "Positive thinking is powerful!" We all can serve by sharing a positive attitude with and toward others.

POSITIVITY IS A CHOICE

We can serve others through our positive attitude. Positivity is a choice we can make every day in most situations. We can choose to be negative, or we can choose to be positive. I personally choose to be positive and see the bright side of things. Choosing to view life, circumstances, and situations from a positive lens helps to keep me motivated. It helps me to focus on serving as an effective father, spouse, community member, and friend. And like many, I am a much better person when my thinking is positive and optimistic.

A negative attitude believes that "sometimes we win, and sometimes we lose." However, having a positive attitude takes on a mindset that we can learn from our losses. The idea here is that we can coach ourselves to think positive. Like any great athletic coach, parent, team member, trainer, or leader, we look at the loss as a learning opportunity to improve, get better, and be prepared for how to overcome a loss when encountering a particular circumstance or situation the next time. When we take on a positive attitude, we choose to be hopeful, positive, and optimistic. As a result, we are equipped to serve others and can help others work through self-doubt, negativity, and giving up.

45

As I stated earlier, great coaches, friends, leaders, parents, and teachers do this every day. Equipped to serve is about helping individuals and groups of people find positivity in situations regardless of favorable or unfavorable outcomes. It is about helping others choose a positive outlook.

POSITIVE REINFORCEMENT

Switching from punishment to positive reinforcement is the best thing you can do for your child's mental health and further development. It does require patience and devotion, but it's one of the best gifts you can give to your child. We've learned a lot about mental health and social-emotional well-being over the past five years. One thing is for sure: yelling, screaming, beating, and punishing our children is not effective. I don't recall ever becoming motivated by a punitive and yelling coach, teacher, or supervisor. Whereas spirited positive reinforcement, whether on the field, in the classroom, or workplace, has proven to be a consistent motivating force that helps all to become their very best.

EQUIPPED TO POSITIVELY SERVE OTHERS

Consider these strategies to serve as a positive influence for others. It is not an all-inclusive list but a starting point as you equip yourself to serve others.

Focus on the positive. Remember the thermostat and the thermometer. Dealing with negative people doesn't mean you have to adjust your mood based on others in the room. You have the option to stay positive.

Use laughter. Most, if not all of us, enjoy a good laugh. Laughter is a great way to lighten up a situation or shift the temperature to a positive vibe.

Compliment Others. Who doesn't enjoy receiving a compliment or affirmation? Sometimes people need to hear something positive about

POSITIVE ATTITUDE TOWARDS OTHERS

themselves to get through a challenging day or situation. However, be sure to provide authentic compliments.

Be Transparent. Sometimes our friends, families and coworkers need to know our stories and how we overcame an obstacle. You may end up serving as hope for someone else.

Be Kind. Acts of random kindness. In the words of my father, "You never lose being kind."

Give Yourself and Others the Benefit of the Doubt. We all make mistakes. I make many mistakes within the first hour of starting my day at times. However, I can also choose to learn from my mistakes and not let them create unneeded stress. I can choose to stay positive.

Check-in. Sometimes people just need someone to see and acknowledge them and let them know things will be okay.

Remember Your Successes. It is okay to reflect on your successes. They may bring you positive motivation.

By living positive, you can serve others and are empowered to make this world a better place.

REFLECTION:

1. What am I most optimistic about after reading this chapter?
2. What can I do to be a better example of a positive person?
3. How can I assist others to become more positive?
4. This week I will exhibit a positive attitude towards_____ (name/activity).

CHAPTER 6

PEOPLE-CENTERED TOWARDS OTHERS

PEOPLE-CENTERED TOWARDS OTHERS - Giving our time and energy to making those we love, serve, and work with an important part of our daily practice. It is acknowledging the human in everyone and everything we do.

The idea of people-centrism, or being people-centered, has gained traction over the past three decades. For the purpose of this chapter, people-centered or people-centric means to give our time and energy to making those we love, serve, and work with an important part of our daily practices. It is acknowledging the human in everyone and everything we do. For example, when you stop by your favorite coffee shop on the way to work and the cashier makes a mistake with your order, how will you respond? Will you model kindness and grace in the situation, or will you erupt?

Although not a new idea, more research on the topic of people-centrism is growing across various industries, and we see the need. For example, in the construction industry, research examines the idea of

PEOPLE-CENTERED TOWARDS OTHERS

people-centered innovation and how shared vision across stakeholders can improve outcomes. In other industries, including education, terms like servant leadership, shared leadership, and culturally responsive leadership also focus on the need to be people centered. In fact, many organizations now days have human resources departments and diversity, equity, and inclusion offices to concentrate on the people working in an organization. Large companies offer research studies on the financial benefits of a people-centered organization. However, whether you work for a corporation or are self-employed, the impact of a global pandemic, international politics, and race and religious relations around the world is reason enough to grow in our efforts to be people-centered and human being focused.

Over the past 30 years, we've learned more about social justice movements and equality because of international peace marches for equity and equality of services, pay, and treatment of people from all backgrounds. But the idea of being people-centered in this chapter is based on what all of us can do as humans regardless of our work titles, political views, fame, or incomes. To be people-centered is to give our time and energy to making those we love, serve, and work with an important part of our daily practices, and to put people literally at the center of everything we do.

In a people-centered environment, those who place people at the center can function at a high level even when the "energy zappers" are active. I served as a director with a team of 25 diverse individuals representing eight different countries at one point in my career. One of my team members was an energy zapper. However, it was amazing to watch the interactions of my team and those who always stayed positive and focused on the needs of the team. The outcome was a genuine trust for each other, safety amongst the team, and a safe space to be transparent away from the "energy zapper." Team members kept each other at the center and cared for each other. John Maxwell, an international thought leader, is quoted as saying, "people don't care how

Equipped to Serve

much you know until they know how much you care." At the heart of a people centered approach is the idea of caring for others, or what Clifton L. Taulbert calls "nurturing attitude."

Throughout history are many examples of individuals who were people centered. Individuals like Mother Teresa, Clarissa H. Barton, and Harriet Tubman highlight how average people became prominent figures in history because of their people centered approach. Mother Teresa, working as a nun, would create the Missionaries of Charity, numbering more than 4,000 members around the world, helping thousands of individuals in need. Clarissa Barton, known as Clara Barton, who worked as a teacher and office clerk, would one day create the American Red Cross, an organization that was founded in 1881 and remains in existence today. During the civil war, prior to her work with the Red Cross, Clara would risk her life to take needed supplies and bandages to soldiers in battle. Harriet Tubman, born into slavery, would one day run away to freedom. During her life, she would become an abolitionist and fight for the freedom of all enslaved people. During her childhood, Tubman watched her siblings be sold to other slave owners, and she would experience physical abuse that would permanently scar her for life. However, she would ultimately help hundreds of enslaved people to freedom by traveling back to enslaved areas using what was known as the Underground Railroad and would later serve as a spy for the Union Army.

Throughout history are stories of individuals like Mother Teresa, Clara Barton and Harriet Tubman giving their time and energy to serving others and acknowledging the human in their work to make our world a better place.

Today there are many others who, in their own way, put people first and acknowledge the human in all that they do. One example is Regina Hart. We've been married for 25 years. Regina grew up as an only child. Some of you reading this chapter may have heard of an outdated phrase called the "only child syndrome." Psychologists G. Stanley Hall

50

PEOPLE-CENTERED TOWARDS OTHERS

and E. W. Bohannon developed their theory in the late 1800s arguing that being an only child was a disease. We know today that their theory was wrong. Regina grew up with her mother Deborah and grandmother, Ms. Juana. Although she did not grow up with siblings, she grew up in a home that opened its living room to members in the community. Regina grew up seeing her grandmother help and serve people. Her grandmother believed that the community was an extension of their family. So, Regina grew up believing that family helps family. She was taught to do unto others as you would like them to do unto you and learned firsthand the Golden Rule principle of treating others the way you want to be treated.

Although her grandmother had only one child, she grew up in a very large family, so Regina's extended family was very large. In addition to Regina's great aunts, uncles, and cousins, her grandmother would invite many others to be part of their community as surrogate aunts, uncles, and cousins. Regina's grandmother's house was never empty. My wife never minded having lots of people over to their home, and especially enjoyed it on holidays. Those family and friends who could not make it to dinner at Ms. Juana's home could stop by and take a plate to go. Ms. Juana would always cook as if she was feeding an army. When she wasn't cooking for friends and family, Ms. Juana owned and operated a hair salon in her basement. There were many times she washed and styled the customers' hair for free because of their financial circumstances. To be people centered starts with building community and relationships. Ms. Juana paid attention to the needs and concerns of family members and clients alike. She was committed to helping and serving others to the best of her ability. She heard the needs of her clients by offering them 100% free discounts for a wash and style. Although Ms. Juana did not own a fortune 500 company, she understood that running a people centered business meant strengthening relationships and trust and creating brand loyalty. She acknowledged the human in each of her customers and family. I share

Equipped to Serve

the story of Regina's grandmother because the people centered actions have continued and are alive and active in Regina. One of our goals as adults and parents should be to always pass down practices that will make our children better people; these lessons transcend time. One of the ways we can serve others is by including our children in service, teaching our children the importance of giving back, and ensuring we keep the human in all of us at the forefront of our work. Empowering others also means empowering our children to empower others. Ms. Juana passed on tools so that Regina would be equipped to serve others, specifically through her people centric mindset.

Today, Regina owns her own insurance agency. She applies the people centered strategies learned from her grandmother. Although her business is insurance, she serves as a listening ear to her clients. Often, she prays for clients experiencing divorce, or loss of a loved one. Many of her clients are in their 80s and have lost family and loved ones. She helps them, of course, with the logistics of their insurance, but in addition, many just needed a listening ear, and she keeps this sense of empathy and compassion at the forefront of her work. In some instances, she has spoken with clients about her faith walk. Inadvertently, by putting the people first before the products and services she is selling, her clients continue to come back, making her business a great success. When we focus on people and not products, our impact is much greater. Often, Regina will turn away business if she knows the client will be better off with their current coverage from another company in the long-term, even though this means she will lose business. Equipped to serve is about putting the needs of others first before your personal gain.

When asked about why she does what she does, she shared, "People need to feel heard and affirmed. They need someone to listen and talk to. We were not designed to live this life alone, so we need someone to talk to. I enjoy helping people and putting people first; it is a rewarding and satisfying experience. Seeing my grandmother help people instilled in me that the greater community is an extension of your family. So, we

PEOPLE-CENTERED TOWARDS OTHERS

are all family. Family helps family. I want to see everyone succeed and reach their full potential. I get satisfaction from seeing others succeed. Do unto others as you would have them do to you."

Two additional examples that highlight Regina's people centered approach is her love of cooking, and when she served as president of a local civic organization. Each year, my wife cooks Christmas Dinner for my family (and sometimes Easter, Thanksgiving, and Just-Because dinners). Although her parents and grandparents have passed away, she believes that cooking a dynamic meal for all to enjoy is one way to make those we love, serve and work with an important part of our daily practices. So, during the holiday season, she "puts her foot into the food" (African American cultural compliment to the chef) and makes my family the most important people in the world. And, while serving as president of a local civic group, she would make hand-made bracelets with a message of kindness for all new members. In both instances, these acts of kindness emphasize building community, showing people you care, and creating appreciation and inclusion. At the heart of people centered work is creating a sense of value and showing that each person in a group matter. Equipped to serve is about giving our time and energy to making those we love, serve, and work with an important part of our daily practice.

WAYS TO MAKE PEOPLE THE PRIORITY

There are many ways we can serve others by making people the priority. For example:

Expressing an attitude of gratitude and appreciation, and valuing others for their contributions to your community, team, or work. We must take time to celebrate the positive qualities demonstrated by our family, friends, and coworkers. If we are not careful, it becomes easy to focus on what is not working well instead of all the things that are working well.

Equipped to Serve

We can serve as an attentive listening ear for someone in need. With modern technology and exponential growth in communication devices to connect us with people around the world, it seems many of us have either forgotten or have not learned how to communicate with someone standing directly in front of us. The idea of listening has become a forgotten or lost art. But, knowing how to listen effectively can bring many positive benefits to ourselves and others. It can strengthen both personal and professional relationships, and boost career opportunities.

Our daily schedules may be very busy, but we should never be too busy to listen to a family member, friend, or coworker in need. I'll admit there were many times I told myself or acted on the belief that I didn't have time to listen. In every instance, had I taken just a moment, an outcome may have been different. For example, maybe my child would have gotten an A+ instead of a B- on an assignment, or maybe a coworker would have decided to stick with an employer instead of leaving, or a mentee may have handled a traumatic situation better. Sometimes a listening ear can be the difference in someone wanting to quit a job, quit school, quit a team, or give up on a valued relationship. No matter how important or how big a title is, we all need a listening ear. An unknown author once said, "If speaking is silver, then listening is gold."

Another way to serve and make people the priority is through generous giving. Whether you are giving time or money, both require a people centered approach to life. For supervisors, giving team members gift cards, special luncheons, paid time off, and hosting events that focus on those you serve, are all good examples of making your team an important part of your daily practice. One of my favorite examples happened during my first year as a school principal – our district superintendent (Roger Pfeiffer) at the time invited all 100+ school leaders to his home. He paid the bill (no corporate budget) and provided all you can eat food, an opportunity for long-needed fellowship, no time limit, and invited our families to participate in the experience. Another

54

PEOPLE-CENTERED TOWARDS OTHERS

example happened during my junior year in college – I, along with several other students, were invited to watch the NBA championship and eat dinner at the home of Dr. Holloway, President of Langston University. None of us students could make it home for the summer, so we stayed on campus. Dr. Holloway cooked freshwater catfish with all the side dishes a college student could want. Afterward, he welcomed us to stop by his office to visit and shared that he would make time for us. For Dr. Holloway, we were more than tuition paying students. We were part of his community, and his people-centered approach is what set that community apart.

A less expensive way to put others first is by treating people with compassion, dignity, and respect. Respect, according to Taulbert, is something understood by all whether you are six, 26 or 86. We should make it a priority to ensure our relationships with others are positive and meaningful, and that we put those relationships and people first in our dealings. We each have more than enough life challenges to tackle daily. Why add to the list of challenges by creating negative relationships with those we encounter daily?

Serving through a caring heart is another way to activate a people centered mindset. When you care for others, you benefit just as much as those you are serving. Based on my research, the benefits of people centeredness can enhance your relationships because you seek to understand others, it increases your ability to form new relationships, your ability to negotiate situations and spaces, and increases your ability to influence others. Again, the power in receiving is giving.

THE STORY OF TWO LANDSCAPERS

I am reminded of a story about two people who worked in landscaping. Joshua and Jordan were landscapers for a large apartment complex. However, something just wasn't right with Joshua. He was under a huge amount of pressure and struggled to get his portion of the complex in

Equipped to Serve

tiptop shape. When his plea for help was ignored, things went from bad to worse. Joshua had fallen behind on his projects and work began to pile up. Jordan, his co-worker, noticed that Joshua seemed worried and stressed during that time, but Jordan didn't want to get involved. "To each their own," Jordan thought. Jordan never wanted to do more than what was required. One day, Joshua reached out to Jordan to ask for help with his area of the apartment complex. Jordan thought about helping for a moment, but she didn't feel like adding more work on top of her own work. Besides, if she helped Joshua, she might have to stay late and decided not to help. Joshua was disappointed, but quickly moved on. Time passed, and Jordan went home at exactly 2 p.m. without noticing Joshua hard at work.

The next day, Jordan noticed Joshua wasn't cleaning the leaves or mowing the grass, so she checked in with her boss to find out Joshua's whereabouts. "He called in and quit," her boss said. "He said the job was too stressful. We'll find a replacement as soon as possible. In the meantime, I'll need you to take on his work as well." In the end, Jordan found herself completing twice the landscaping as Joshua and the work began to pile up. Jordan thought to herself, "I should have helped him." The moral of the story is to be willing to help others because you may need help one day. Making those you serve the priority and at the center of your service will not only benefit the others, but also yourself.

Whether you serve in church ministry, corporate America, or in public service, acknowledging the human in everyone and everything we do will pay dividends in the long run.

REFLECTION:

1. In what ways can I give my time to make my family life more harmonious?
2. How do I demonstrate putting others first?
3. What is one activity or strategy I will employ to show my co-workers they are a priority?

PEOPLE-CENTERED TOWARDS OTHERS

CHALLENGE:

Start each day thinking about who you can serve because of your position in the community, church, home, or work. Reflect on how you can put people first in what you will do that day.

CHAPTER 7

EXAMPLE FOR OTHERS

EXAMPLE FOR OTHERS - Giving others the best of who you are while serving as a role model to imitate and duplicate by others.

To be an example is to be a model or the standard. In this case, an example is a role model. To be clear, a role model is not a perfect person, but instead, a positive example of how to live and do things. Now more than ever, we need empowered people to empower others, and to step up and serve as examples for current and future generations. What better way to serve others than to be an example of what can be?

> *Now more than ever, we need empowered people to empower others.*

In my lifetime, I've had the good fortune of having several men and women willingly serve as an example of what can be possible for me.

EXAMPLE FOR OTHERS

In chapter two, I highlight my mother's focus on quality time. In addition to my mother, several other women were equipped to serve as an example for me. In elementary school, and in high school, I was fortunate to have teachers who served as positive examples – Mrs. Summers and Mrs. Lewis, who were best friends, served as my second and third-grade teachers, respectively. Both teachers modeled high expectations and the importance of learning your heritage. In high school, Mrs. Taylor served as my geometry teacher. She would instill in me the importance of being on-time and taking responsibility for completing assignments. She had high expectations and would hold me accountable. In fact, during my junior year in high school, a time when I thought I was "bigger than my britches," Mrs. Taylor was my only teacher to hold me to high expectations and would communicate with my parents. I never wanted her to call my home, so I chose to do my best and be my best. Her example of a teacher held true when I chose a career path serving as a classroom teacher. In my first year of teaching, I had 22 eighth grade girls in my first period class, and not one boy student. We had a great year, and I continued the high standard of teaching and learning that was shared with me. In fact, one of my students, Rhea, recently reminded me of her experience during my first year of teaching, and a statement I shared with her over twenty-five years ago when she was a seventh grader. Rhea shared that she showed up for class unprepared one day and that I stopped her in the hallway and stated, "You come to my class not prepared." Ms. Rhea would later share that I taught her a life lesson in the hallway outside of my classroom that day. Rhea was part of my Technology Student Association (TSA) club and would participate in tech competitions. Today she has her master's degree in information systems and works in the tech industry. The impact on Rhea's success started with Ms. Taylor holding me accountable as a student and serving as an example, so I could serve as an example later in my life for Rhea.

In my lifetime, I have benefited from multiple male role models

Equipped to Serve

as well. Some were from a peripheral perspective while others were equipped to serve in a mentor-mentee relationship. As a college student attending Langston University, Dr. Hedge and Dr. Johnson served as dynamic examples of how to equip and serve college students to be their best. Harold Helton and Donovan Bowers hired me as an intern at the Oklahoma Department of Career and Technical Education State Office. I had very little in common with both gentlemen. However, they saw my potential and equipped me to serve as a technology teacher in the school Rhea attended.

My father is my greatest example of what it means to be equipped to serve. My father, Dwight Hart, was born during the baby boomer years. He would emulate his life after the example my grandfather, Sylvester Hart, set before him. My grandfather, part of the silent generation, instilled in my father patience, persistence, loyalty, sacrifice, selflessness, hard work and a commitment to family. My grandfather would also instill in my father to reach for the stars and pursue his dreams. Like my grandfather, civil rights leaders like Dr. Martin L. King, Jr., and the Little Rock Nine – students who integrated Central High School – came out of the silent generation. These individuals would serve as beacons of hope for the entire world.

My grandfather did not attend school until he was 10 years old and got no further than the third grade. However, he would migrate from Oklahoma and Arkansas doing farm work to become an expert drafter in Arizona at a time when few Black men served as expert drafters. Although my grandfather did not attend college, eight of his eleven children would attend college and complete a degree due to his influence and example of strong work ethic.

For my father, his father served as an example for him to duplicate. Consequently, my father was driven to serve as the same type of example for his family. He would cultivate the idea of serving others by his example. My father was molded into the person he is today because of growing up in the 50's and 60's. By default, he served as an example to

60

EXAMPLE FOR OTHERS

his siblings. The oldest of eleven, he went to college, and nine siblings followed even when it was not the norm in society to do so. While in college in the late 60's, he experienced a mixed bag of opportunities full of expectations and racism. What motivated him was the idea of being the first in his family and one of the first in his community to attend college. A small percentage of African Americans attending his high school would go on to college because they did not receive much guidance or support to pursue education past high school. He would notice this same type of lack during his path for career opportunities and promotion. While in college, there were situations he expected and did not expect to encounter. For example, completing rigorous coursework and learning new information was an expectation. However, learning about computers in the 60s was a challenge as he had never seen a computer or written computer code like Fortran during high school. Other challenges centered on diversity. The university he attended had close to 25,000 students and 175 were identified as African American. Of the 175 African American students, most were on athletic scholarship at the time. My father was one of the only, if not the only, African American in the College of Mines which housed the chemical engineering degree program. His goal was to become an engineer and serve as an example to his community.

Unfortunately, his goal was derailed after his first year in college. At the end of his first year, he finished seventh in a class of about 45 students. However, his advisor told him that he did not have the aptitude to be an engineer. That same advisor would inform my father that he was receiving too much financial aid and would revoke his top 5% graduation and residency scholarships. My father would not graduate with an engineering degree. However, decades later, after starting a family, he would live out the character traits of persistence and hard work modeled by his father and would eventually complete his master's degree and retire from a large missile systems company as a systems engineer. He would experience similar challenges in his career.

61

Equipped to Serve

To be an engineer he was told he had to have a degree. However, during his tenure he would train co-workers with no degree to later find out they were promoted to the title of engineer. The only difference between himself and them was that they were not from marginalized communities. From that perspective, it was important for him to be an example that defied the odds. He would later advocate for himself to be an engineer and was given an opportunity to create and teach incoming assemblers techniques around manufacturing. In his words, "part of setting an example for my family and self was finishing that which I had started, knowing I could do it, regardless of the circumstances I encountered in the late 60s or at work. One thing about serving as an example is that the cost is not free. There is always a cost, and it will cost, but it was a price I was willing to pay." His example of completion would impact my siblings and me to all pursue higher education, with two of us achieving post bachelor's degrees.

Beyond schooling and work, my father served as an example and role model to others in our community. He served as a volunteer teacher in our local church community for 40 years and served as a math tutor helping students in elementary and middle school. Serving as a volunteer tutor for students historically underserved allowed him to live out "giving others the best of who you are while serving as a role model." His tutoring support would serve as an avenue to help young men stay on track academically in order to pursue their dreams. Several of the young men he helped academically were my childhood friends and schoolmates who would go on to attend college, become professional athletes, and even become an Olympic medalist. For my dad, tutoring gave him the chance to serve as a mentor and ensure a group of students would have academic success. The time with young students was for homework help, making connections, showing students a vision of who they could become, and serving as a fatherly example. In America, over eighteen million children grow up without a father figure at home. I would have also fell into the same fatherlessness had

EXAMPLE FOR OTHERS

it not been for my father. I shared in a prior chapter that according to my biological father, a relationship that has been restored in my adulthood, he called my father, "The man I was not able to be." Today, both men are an example of restored relationships and two men sharing fatherhood together. Dwight Hart is my father, and JD Hill (Pops) is my biological father. Their example of brotherhood, friendship, and shared fatherhood is an example for others to emulate. Equipped to serve means that we give others our best while serving as a role model.

LEADING BY EXAMPLE

We all can lead by example regardless of our titles, position, and education status. Each day we have an opportunity to show up as our best self. Simply by showing up as our best self, we may never know who we have become a role model for. Every day we have an opportunity to serve others by our example. Do we give off positive energy or are we always negative? Do I promote and listen to negative talk about others, or do I lead by example and put a stop to it? Our example can be a model for how others deal with conflict, and how to handle challenges in a positive way.

Everyday Example

Taking a page from the silent generation years, we all have the opportunity serve others through our daily lives. We make a choice to be enthusiastic and do our best each day, to exhibit a strong work ethic, be authentic and be of honest character, to exhibit patience and persistence, loyalty, selflessness, and a hard-working mindset. We choose to "walk the walk" and allow our actions to match our words.

If you are a parent, leading by example is one of the best ways to serve your children. In fact, our goal as parents should be to serve as great examples for our children, to live out the attributes in

63

Equipped to Serve

this book in a way that our children will want to emulate. Stephen Covey was known to say, "What you do has a far greater impact than what you say." Today, more than ever, we need parents to make the choice to be a positive example for their own children as well as other's children.

REFLECTION:

1. What makes me a good example?
2. What am I great at that makes me an example?
3. How can I use my own growth to help others be their best?
4. How can I lead by example?
5. Who do I serve through my example every day?

CHAPTER 8

DEVELOP OTHERS

DEVELOP OTHERS - Seeing someone's potential and providing coaching, support, opportunities to grow, learn and succeed.

Over the years, there has been much discussion around the topic of leaders developing others. For example, Zig Zigler shared, "Successful people use their strength by recognizing, developing, and utilizing the talents of others." Harvey S. Firestone, creator of Firestone Tires once stated, "It is only as we develop others that we permanently succeed." For both Zigler and Firestone, developing others was part of their formula for success.

Much of the research on this topic centers on workplace strategies for leaders and managers to develop and aid their staff in taking on future leadership positions. The topic of workplace employee development is one that will impact all of us whether we serve in leadership or serve in an employee subordinate role. However, for the purpose of this chapter, the idea of serving by developing others applies to all of us regardless of work titles, positions, income, and education. We all have the ability to develop someone else. Developing others through service is about seeing someone's potential and providing coaching, support, opportunities to grow, learn and succeed. Take, for example,

65

Equipped to Serve

a co-worker who teaches a new team member how to use the organizations data monitoring systems, or a sibling sharing a lesson learned, or a parent developing her child's ability to cope with a challenge, we all have an opportunity to serve by developing others.

In my line of work as an educator, developing others is a badge of honor. To see people who I was given an opportunity to lead and serve reach the same level of achievement and surpass me in their work is very rewarding and satisfying. I led by example, but also actively sought out this potential and coached these individuals through to achieving their goals. Also rewarding, was giving individuals a project that stretched their skills and required new learning. Once they successfully completed their project, I enjoyed stepping to the back so they could enjoy the benefits of serving as the lead. Regardless of your role, whether it be a schoolteacher, high school principal, school district leader, corporate executive, garbage worker or housekeeper, we all have the capability to develop others.

When we develop others, we create greater purpose for ourselves, and we positively impact the life of someone else, and potentially future generations. Take, for example, my grandparents, Sylvester, and Martha Hart. Born in the small town of Bristow, Oklahoma, during the 1920's, my grandfather, on the tail end of the greatest generation, and my grandmother, at the beginning of the silent generation, both understood the importance of developing others. Although neither completed college, and my grandfather only completed a few years of grammar school, they raised eleven children to value education. My grandparents grew up in an era when few African Americans were allowed and able to attend non-Black colleges and universities. But they made it a point to actively engage in each of their children's schooling and rewarded hard work and academic success. They assisted with homework and relied on the older siblings to help their younger siblings. The result was that nine of their eleven children attended college and completed an associates, bachelors, masters, or doctorate degree.

DEVELOP OTHERS

That same value for education was passed down to their grandchildren, who completed an associates or higher degree. The investment my grandparents made in their children was passed down to their grandchildren, and great grandchildren. Without the investment from my grandparents in developing their children to acquire an opportunity they never had, they may not have seen the opportunity or value in education, and generations of my family would have a different story. Equipped to serve is about developing others potential and providing coaching, support, opportunities to grow, learn and succeed. My grandparents were the epitome of investing time and effort into helping someone grow, learn, and succeed. Like my grandparents, we all can invest time and effort into someone else.

There is a somewhat familiar quote that was prevalent during my grandparents' time. The quote was often shared with youth and states, "Do as I say, and not as I do." Writers have argued the meaning of the quote and promoted various meanings; however, I interpret the quote as saying that one's words don't match their actions. I pulled the "Do as I say" quote into this conversation on developing others because to develop someone else involves modeling the right practice, as we discussed in the previous chapter about serving as an example. The idea here is that someone is always watching us, and we have an opportunity to develop others through our actions. Whether you are a pro athlete, government official, entertainer or a parent coaching a little league team, someone is watching how we develop others, and they are watching your actions. In short, people, and lots of young people, are watching and learning from our actions and behavior more than our words.

As you've likely gathered from my referencing sports repeatedly, I do watch a good number of sports, and in particular football. I often find inspiration from incredible individuals who are equipped to serve within the athletics community. One example of developing others is former Louisiana State University and current Alabama University head coach Nick Saban. Coach Saban has led his teams to a total of seven national championship titles at the time of writing this chapter. However, just as impressive is his development of future head coaches. Coach Saban has developed nine former assistant coaches to become head coaches at the college level, and at least one has won a national college football championship.[10] Coach Saban chose to not only focus on his own personal success in the coaching arena, but also to turn his talents toward developing future coaches. This shows a genuine care and desire to serve and support others, and the future of the sport as a whole, as opposed to just his personal gain. He saw others' potential and provided support, opportunities to grow, learn, and succeed. Equipped to serve is about empowering others for success.

Whether good or bad, someone is always watching you and learning from your behavior. Someone I have watched for more than 20 years, as you may have gathered from my speaking about his work at length, is Clifton L. Taulbert. Clifton serves as a mentor and guide who develops others directly and indirectly. For me, he has served as a mentor providing direct and indirect coaching, support, opportunities to grow, learn and succeed. Throughout this book I have given several ideas for how we all can serve to develop others – inspiration, empowerment, the gift of time, and unselfish acts of random kindness. Mr. Taulbert has, at some point over the past 20 years, modeled each of the characteristics outlined in this book and used the characteristics to develop others.

I first met Clifton after hearing him speak on building community during a multicultural symposium I attended. The symposium was recommended as part of my Master of Education program during my time in Oklahoma City, OK. His presentation style and ideas about community and diversity were inclusive of everyone in attendance. Mr. Taulbert would ultimately serve as my mentor providing opportunities for me to lead workshops and trainings, and travel on behalf of his company. It was during my time working under his mentorship and

DEVELOP OTHERS

leadership that I would understand the importance of spending time with individuals different than me, the emphasis on valuing people, and learning to dig deeper into timeless characteristics that he valued – dependability, responsibility, and hope, amongst other timeless characteristics found in his book The Eight Habits of the Heart.[11] I learned from Clifton the importance of understanding how our character and aspects of our character can and should transcend race, gender, social, economic status, shifts in technology, changes in popular culture, and the latest fad sweeping the country.

While working under Clifton's leadership he would create opportunities for me to practice what I learned and apply that practice in real-time scenarios. Allowing me to lead a section of a workshop and ultimately trusting me to lead a full-day workshop. He was committed to my growth as a trainer and would provide feedback on areas I could improve and gave new strategies to apply. Furthermore, he provided a nurturing environment to take risk and grow. He did not solely focus on his own success as a speaker and coach, but directly participated in developing those that he provided mentorship for, and genuinely caring about the success of others.

Clifton, born in the Mississippi Delta, was the child of a cotton field worker and grew up in an era when discussing race relations was considered forbidden. He would ultimately become an international best-selling author and builder of community. His example affirms regardless of how we grew up and the environment we lived in, or how we live financially, we all can develop others.

Developing others is more than telling people what to do. It is about modeling, being an example, and giving your time to help someone succeed at achieving a desired goal or task. As the famous Chinese Proverb states, "Give a man a fish, and you feed him for a day. Teach a man to fish, and you feed him for a lifetime." Developing others to fish for a lifetime is the daily work of educators around the globe from pre-school to college. It is also the work of every parent raising a child

Equipped to Serve

and so many others who serve in a role designed to cultivate others. But everyone can do this work in their various environments – if you see the potential in someone, help them and become their mentor. You could have an enormous impact on their life.

HOW WE DEVELOP OTHERS

Throughout this book I have given examples and ways to develop others. We are all capable of unselfishly giving our time, inspiring, empowering, and positively serving others. Some ways Clifton Taulbert has taken time to develop me, and others, is through a nurturing attitude, being dependable, and providing hope through his example. As I have stated since the beginning of this chapter, developing others requires seeing someone's potential and providing coaching, support, opportunities to grow, learn and succeed.

Clifton cultivated a passion in me to serve others through his time invested in me, through the many lessons he shared, taught, and modeled, and then by giving me the opportunity to apply what I had learned. He fertilized and watered a desire in me to live out the timeless values of integrity, responsibility, dependability, hope, brotherhood, and nurturing attitude. Each characteristic had already been planted in me by my parents. But, as a young man in my mid-twenties, full of energy and dreams, Clifton took the time to cultivate what he coined "The Eight Habits of the Heart" in me. In Clifton's words, "You are driven by your belief that you are investing knowledge for a future return." To develop others is an empowering example of unselfish service.

If you serve in a leadership position, one of the fastest ways to develop others is through trust. Organization success and leadership development moves at the speed of trust according to Stephen M. R. Covey.[12] Another fast way to develop those you lead is to delegate opportunities to serve in a leadership role. Delegation allows those you develop the opportunity to demonstrate what they've learned and to

DEVELOP OTHERS

be accountable for the opportunity provided to them. Much like Mr. Clifton Taulbert giving me an opportunity to represent his company in multiple states providing leadership development and building community training.

Developing Children

As I stated previously, someone is always watching us. Now, whether we agree or not, we are already investing time and effort into developing someone else. The question becomes are we serving as a positive role model or a negative role model? Children are always watching our actions as parents, grandparents, educators, church leaders, and coaches. For example, children watch the interactions between their parents, parents and teachers, parents and coaches, and other adults that they encounter. Their development and social interactions are based on the daily experiences they observe and witness. If we, as adults, model appropriate adult interactions and place our families at the forefront of positive interactions, our children are likely to develop the same skills. Developing our children is a sure way to stop the idea that "hurt people, hurt people."

Feedback From Those I Have Developed

I believe it is important not only to talk the talk, but to also walk the walk. Below are a few comments from people I was given an opportunity to serve in a developer capacity.

Anonymous - Assistant Principal: "When I was a classroom teacher, I often pondered the idea of being a school administrator. And throughout my certification process, I had many questions about what it would entail to be an administrator. On numerous occasions, Jimmy Hart would give me guidance, wisdom, feedback, and recommendations about his time as a school principal. This information was paramount as it gave me a better understanding of what to expect and how

Equipped to Serve

to navigate through certain situations. Jimmy Hart is always willing to share his knowledge and personal experiences as a mentor and as a friend. And I experienced this sharing firsthand from Jimmy Hart."

David - Television Account Executive: "The value of a Father, Mentor, and leader in a young man's life is truly indispensable. Jimmy is all those and more! He has shown me through mentorship the importance of faith, family, good character, integrity, and hard work. Thank you for being a model."

Gideon – Payroll Senior Analyst: "Jimmy has been more than a big brother. He has been a positive influence in my life and amazing mentor. He keeps it real, listens, does not judge and helps you think things through. He is someone I can always depend on for great advice in any situation."

Trehon – Computer Engineer: "It's not every day a kid moves from his hometown to start a career in a city where he does not know anyone and is treated like family. Now that kid is a husband, father of two, and community advocate in the city which he was embraced. This is what happens when you meet Jimmy Hart. I am forever grateful to be influenced, impacted, and inspired as your mentee and spiritual son."

Developing others is about seeing someone's potential and providing coaching, support, opportunities to grow, learn and succeed. We are all capable of developing another person – you simply need to look around in your life for who might need your support.

REFLECTION:

Who are you developing to take your place at work or in the community?

How are you developing those you lead? Whether it be your children, those you teach or lead, or those you serve at church and in the community, what are you doing to develop others?

CHALLENGE:

DEVELOP OTHERS

Identify one person in your circle who you can serve as a mentor developer. Reach out to the person by phone (text or call) in the next day and begin discussing how you would like to serve as a mentor.

CHAPTER 9

KINDNESS: THE X-FACTOR

"In a world where you can be anything, be kind."
–Unknown

ALTHOUGH KINDNESS IS not one of the words used to describe how we can serve others, I believe it is at the heart of how we serve. I consider kindness the X-factor. Without kindness, it is difficult to serve others authentically. When searching Merriam-Webster Dictionary online, kindness is defined as the quality or state of being kind. Adjectives that describe the word kind in terms of how we treat others are caring, generous, thoughtful, kindhearted, and humanitarian. Kindness requires each of us to do something for someone else.

Activists, political leaders, and entertainers have all chimed in on the idea of kindness. Abraham Lincoln, sixteenth President of the United States, is quoted as saying, "Kindness is the only service that will stand the storm of life and not wash out. It will wear well and will be remembered long after the prism of politeness or the complexion of courtesy has faded away." Maya Angelou, fine arts icon, activist, and

KINDNESS: THE X-FACTOR

scholar, stated, "People will forget what you said, people will forget what you did, but they will never forget how you made them feel." Both Lincoln and Angelou's quotes bring to light the long-term and lasting impact of kindness.

Academic scholars have researched the benefits of kindness for years, and what seems to be an increased interest in kindness over the past 20 to 30 years. Through research, many scholars argue that acts of kindness can improve a person's overall well-being. In a study conducted by Yale and UCLA scholars, and published in the Clinical Psychological Science journal, researchers highlight the personal benefits of helping others and the potential boost in an individual's overall well-being.[13]

My favorite quote on kindness is one shared by my father during a turbulent season in my life. While in my mid-twenties, I experienced a particularly challenging situation and was not sure how to move forward. My attitude had become one of bitterness and anger. During a phone conversation with my father, he said, "You never lose being kind." Those words and the way he articulated the idea of kindness has stuck with me forever. The idea that even in your most challenging situation, and when you feel like you are on the losing end, we all have a choice to exhibit kindness. Fast forward to the present, and after living through many more challenging circumstances and challenging

> # "You never lose being kind."
>
> – Dwight Hart

Equipped to Serve

interactions, the idea that "you never lose being kind" has proven to be 100-percent true.

We have the choice to be kind regardless of our circumstances. Kindness can be a powerful weapon for good. Kindness can build community across generations, race, ethnicity, social economic status, and lifestyle. You may remember in an earlier chapter, I shared the story about my son when he was in third grade, and a student called him the N-word. My son was shocked and confused. However, Sean, a young man in fifth grade, stood up for my son. Sean was not African American but understood what was happening was wrong. His act of random kindness will always be with my family and showed my son we can all choose to be kind. It would have been quite easy for Sean to walk away from the situation. Instead, he chose to take the situation head-on and advocate on behalf of someone in need. My son and Sean would go on to be friends. When we choose kindness, we level up our ability to take the higher road despite what is happening to us by others.

Kindness can be found all around us each day, and everywhere we go, we simply must look for it. In my community, I see kindness all around me. From students hosting fundraisers to help others in need, community groups organizing shoe drives, local police departments hosting backpack and school supply drives, to local churches working tirelessly to serve those with food insecurities throughout the year. During the height of the pandemic in 2020, I witnessed our local mass transportation company provide free bus passes to the entire community, national fitness facilities host free sports camps for youth, and professional athletes donate thousands of dollars during the holidays. On a smaller scale, I witnessed a local gym owner, Bobby Rodriguez of Jet Athletics, host free sports camps and recognition events for local athletes. I witnessed siblings share kind words, parents speaking a positive message into their children's lives, and neighbors helping neighbors. I witnessed my daughter partner with a local community center to donate proceeds from a

KINDNESS: THE X-FACTOR

t-shirt design in support of the center, and my son has taken time to assist younger athletes in their skill development. Throughout this book, I have shared multiple examples of people's kindness and ways to be kind that we may all learn from and apply in our own lives.

GRATEFUL NOT GRAPEFRUIT

To be grateful is to be appreciative and thankful, especially when someone has demonstrated an act of random kindness towards you. Gratitude is where community comes into practice because there are times each of us may be in a position to help someone, and other times when someone else can help us in ways we may not be able to help ourselves.

To be grateful and not grapefruit means to leave bitterness behind. For many, eating grapefruit leaves a bitter taste in one's mouth and is hard to swallow, much like the bitter taste of an ungrateful person can be hard to swallow. According to Seth Meyers, Doctor of Psychology, "As frustrating and negativistic as bitter men and women can be, summon your patience and compassion and remember that happy people – those who feel loved, cared for, and respected – aren't negative and don't mistreat or upset others as a pattern. The bitter man or woman – again, though they'd never admit it – must emotionally hold and carry an overwhelming amount of anger, sadness, and disappointment, and they often secretly feel anger toward themselves, and are enslaved by it."[14] In short, it's important to constantly work on kindness and be kind towards others. We may all remember my father's words: "You never lose being kind."

COMMITMENT:

Commit to becoming a RAKtivist. RAKtivist is short for "Random Acts of Kindness activist." According to the Random Acts of Kindness

Equipped to Serve

Foundation (www.randomactsofkindness.org), a RAKtivist is someone who makes kindness the norm.

Connect with someone close to you and commit to implementing one kind act per month for a person or small group.

CHAPTER 10

WHO WE SERVE

SO FAR, WE'VE discussed the many ways in which we can serve in our homes, on our job or at school, and in the communities we live. This chapter highlights who we serve, the people that all this development work is truly for.

Although we are inundated with mass media and social media highlighting self-absorption, putting our individuality first, or "outshining" someone else, we were born to serve others. Serving others' lives within our DNA. Think about how little children are so eager to help with chores or take on their big brother/sister role. I can recall being excited the first time I got to wash the dishes, as were my children before their teen years, because we inherently enjoy the idea of helping others. The point is, we have service in our make-up as a part of who we are. I remember walking to school as a child in third grade with my sister. My sister was in the first grade. During the rainy time of the year, a particular street would flood, and it was the only route we knew to get to school. Because I was older and taller, I would put my sister on my back as she would hold on tight to my neck to walk across the flooded street with our classmates. At the time, I didn't know I was being of service to my sister. I just knew it was the right thing to do. It

79

Equipped to Serve

is a circumstance that the two of us will always remember, and I have pulled the story out of memory on several occasions over the years to remind her how much I love her during a joking moment. But many of us lose this sense of service as we grow older. It is already within us; we just need to continue cultivating it.

My childhood example shows the importance and value of serving family. In my work as a supervisor, I would always remind my teams that "family is always first." While it is an easy statement to share, and a great way to remind your teams that you value them as individuals, as a leader, it is very easy to not practice what we preach. Family should always have priority over work or anything else on earth. Our family, our loved ones, and relatives, in most situations are the folks who will be by our side no matter what the circumstance or situation. We should always serve our families with our best. People often say, "we put our best foot forward in public;" in other words, those we communicate with on Facebook, at work, and in the community usually see the best of who we are. I recommend a different approach – our families deserve and should be the people who see the best of who we are each day.

Another way to serve our family, friends and others is through our faith. For me, serving through my faith is a way to live out the best of who I am every day. When I apply each of the eight characteristics highlighted in how we serve, I exemplify my faith while serving as an example, and serving others through my actions.

Because we are communal beings, we must also serve our friends. In this case, those closest to us and a part of our inner circle. Whether it be a kind word, a listening ear during a challenging situation, providing a helping hand, taking care of their children for a date night, or serving as an accountability partner, our friends deserve our service. We all need a tribe, a community to serve, to support, and to be supported by.

We are all connected as humans and have many opportunities to serve our fellow brother and sister as part of humanity. Whether you

WHO WE SERVE

are a church leader, corporate executive, or the neighbor three doors down the street, valuing and getting to know people we don't always associate with is a form of service. Take time to get to know something about their background. After all, you may be of benefit to them, but they may also be of service to you.

While serving others is part of our purpose on earth, we must never forget to serve ourselves. I'm sure most people reading this book can think of someone who seems to have left this earth too soon because they never took time to care for themselves while serving others. Often, during my years as an educator, a laughing joke would circulate, stating, "I don't want to be the one person people say, he or she was a great person, we will miss them, but now we must move on." While not really a laughing matter, the statement would remind us that we must be good stewards of ourselves as well as others. Taking care of self does not mean selfishness, it just means we value "sharpening the saw" to stay healthy, refreshed, and constantly growing, improving, and getting better. We must take care of ourselves to be equipped to serve as best as we possibly can. As they say, you cannot pour from an empty cup, so you must fill your cup first.

Below are examples of ways to positively impact WHO we serve.

102 WAYS TO SERVE OTHERS

Family (Loved Ones)

1. Put you family needs first as often as possible. Ensure your family's social and emotional well-being are in good shape.
2. Listen as often as possible to the dreams and aspirations of your loved ones.
3. Be the first to apologize.
4. Write a thank you note, or just a quick note to say I see you. A sticky note works well to say, "great job in school" or "thanks for helping with chores."

81

Equipped to Serve

5. Randomly call, visit, or video conference with a family member you have not spoken to in over six months.

6. Serve as a role model in your home first. In general, I believe people put their best foot forward in public. I encourage you to put your best foot forward at home.

7. Check in on your parents as often as possible. Many people don't have the opportunity to check in on their parents. To have living parents is a blessing.

8. Participate in a community service experience with your children.

9. Volunteer in your child's classroom at least once per year.

10. Serve as a volunteer chaperone for your child's school.

11. Pray as a family; lead your family in prayer.

12. Highlight all the good things in your family. We sometimes focus our celebrations on big accomplishments and miss out on the everyday good that can be taken for granted.

13. Read a book together as a family.

14. Take a road trip. Sometimes getting outside and to the local park can lift everyone's spirit.

15. Text a thank you and an I love you as often as possible.

16. Be slow to yell. Yelling usually doesn't work for anyone.

17. Teach your children the importance of serving others.

18. Model how to serve others for your children.

19. Bring back eating as a family. Research shares that less than 40% of families eat together, although family mealtime is beneficial to children K-18.

20. Give a gift just because. It doesn't matter if their birthday was last week or six months from now.

Fellowship (Community)

21. Invite a neighbor over for dinner. If you are uncomfortable inviting them into your home, meet them at a local restaurant.

WHO WE SERVE

22. Serve as a mentor to someone wanting to grow in an area you have experience and a proven track record.
23. Advocate on behalf of someone less fortunate and in need.
24. Volunteer in your local school, youth center, or church.
25. Volunteer to speak, work, or cook meals at a homeless shelter.
26. Serve as a mentor to a youth living in a group home.
27. Purchase books for nearby elementary schools. Find out what the school needs before you purchase.
28. If your children play sports – be the parent that yells positivity. We have more than enough parents who yell, curse, and scream at the coaches and referees.
29. Thank a service worker for their work. This includes teachers, teacher assistants, bus drivers, housekeeping at hotels and all others in a service field.
30. When checking out of a hotel, tip your housekeeper.
31. Donate blood when an opportunity is provided. You may not feel comfortable going to a blood bank or plasma center, but when the Red Cross shows up at your church, school, or work, consider donating to help people in need.
32. Volunteer at a community center for veterans.
33. Help with voter registration.
34. Tutor elementary students in reading after school.
35. Participate in a community beautification project. For example, adding safe playground equipment and debris cleanup at a school or park could be helpful.
36. Read poetry to residents living in a retirement community.
37. Donate to your local food bank.
38. Sign up for a local, national, or international mission trip.
39. If you are a student, start a club that addresses a need at your school.
40. Serve at your local crisis center.

Equipped to Serve

41. Host a holiday meal for college student unable to go home. Reach out to the student services office at your local college.
42. Donate quality clothing to the clothing bank. We all have stuff in our closet we've been saving to wear or is no longer part of our rotation. Share some of the good stuff.

Formal Work (Career/Job)

43. Smile and greet people regardless of their demeanor.
44. Whether you are a leader in charge of serving your team or a co-worker, a gift card for a cup of coffee or lunch is an unselfish act of service.
45. Take on a leadership opportunity – leading or spearheading a project is a great way to serve others.
46. Be an encourager. Lift people up and speak positive thoughts into their life. We all love encouragement.
47. Stay positive. Negative energy slows down everything positive.
48. Get to know a co-worker beyond what they do at work. The more we know about each other, and each other's culture, the less afraid and assuming we will be.
49. Congratulate others on their successes.
50. Avoid gossip. Remember that the person telling you all the gossip is also gossiping about you. Encourage the person to go talk with who they are gossiping about. You both will be better off in the long run…no need to carry falsehoods around that someone gave you about someone else. I don't know about you, but I have enough on my plate already.
51. Build community by promoting diversity of voice, perspective, and inclusion.
52. Be kind. I've shared my father's words with you – "you never lose being kind."
53. Don't be judgmental. We all have value.

WHO WE SERVE

54. Apologize if you are wrong or made a mistake. We all make mistakes.
55. Give grace…we are all navigating life, and life's challenges daily.
56. Serve as a mentor if you can help someone grow or move into a growth opportunity.
57. Pick two of the how we serve characteristics from this book to practice daily.
58. Celebrate those who keep the workspace and restrooms clean. We learned their value during the Covid-19 pandemic.
59. Develop a community service project to support a local school or non-profit. For example, an entire office team taking time to read to students at an elementary.
60. Unselfishly help a colleague working to complete a big project or meet a deadline.
61. Build in a service opportunity if one does not exist for your employer.
62. Acts of random kindness are always a great way to serve others.
63. Serve as an inspirer. Share a motivational quote or video before a team meeting.
64. Be friendly to those who seem to always exhibit negativity and may even exhibit rudeness. Your kindness may be what is needed to change the negative recording playing in their brain.

Friendship (Inner Circle)
65. Listen to their concerns and challenges without giving a solution. Sometimes a friend just needs to know you care enough about them to just listen.
66. Apologize quickly and sincerely when you make a mistake. Pride has destroyed many friendships.
67. Be honest. Good friends help each other get better.

Equipped to Serve

68. Be patient. We don't all grow, interpret, and understand how to live life the exact same way.
69. Give grace. We all need it.
70. Help with a personal project if you live in the area.
71. Donate to a cause important to your friend.
72. Be the first to congratulate when someone from your inner circle receives an award or reach a goal that was shared with you.
73. Setup a Zoom or Facetime call to let them know you were thinking about them.
74. Sometimes just let them have the floor to discuss whatever they want. No need to compete for talking time. Afterall, they are your friend.
75. You can never go wrong with an unexpected gift.
76. Follow-through in times of need. A prayer is good, but a prayer and lending hand is even better.

Faith (Spiritual Walk)

77. Share your faith with someone. We all need hope in our life.
78. Pray for someone in need. Ask what you can pray about for them and on their behalf…don't assume you know what they need.
79. Inspire others through your faith walk and example. You'll be surprised how many people will consider learning more about your faith based on how they see you react in different types of difficult situations.
80. Don't take yourself so seriously. Let your light shine so others may see an example of what good looks like.
81. Slow down to listen (yes this takes discipline).
82. Model your faith even in the face of disrespect. You're not a floor mat, but you can address the situation with grace, kindness, and respectfully. No need to stoop to other people's lows.

WHO WE SERVE

83. Share your talents and giftings with others.
84. Pray for your friends and family. Whether it be a friend applying to a new position, or a family member struggling, there is power in prayer.
85. Enact the simple but challenging act of loving your neighbor.
86. Invest in others through your faith. "Love your neighbor as yourself."

Finance (Money)

87. Donate to a local charity or school program.
88. Pay it forward. The power in receiving is giving.
89. Donate to a local church program to help families in need.
90. Buy a few packs of new socks for your local food bank or homeless shelter.
91. Fund a ministry project locally, nationally, or internationally.
92. Give away several nice items of clothing or other belongings you haven't used in several years.
93. Lone without expecting anything in return. This can be a challenge. But if you lone someone money, do so out of kindness and support. If they give it back, it is a blessing. If you don't have it to give, help the person brainstorm a solution. Sometimes people just need a little help with figuring out the how.
94. Give without having your name announced. Giving is a great way to serve others, and we don't have to always broadcast our gift.
95. Purchase food at least once a year for the homeless in your city. No selfies, please…Stay humble.

Fitness (Whole Self)

96. Self-reflect. Spend time thinking about where you are in life and where you want to be in one year.

Equipped to Serve

97. Proper sleep. It is okay to sleep in sometimes or go to bed early to get in those 8 or so hours, which are so important for our health and well-being.

98. Sharpen the saw, learn something new. Sometimes learning a new skill gives us new energy and maintaining an attitude of curiosity is a great way to approach the world.

99. Exercise – even just 15 minutes per day while watching the news before bed.

100. Put down your cell phone sooner than later each night. Most of us have probably watched a news clip or read the benefits of disconnecting from our technology at night.

101. Model the equipped to serve attributes for your personal benefit. For example, look in the mirror each day and inspire yourself – what is your daily affirmation?

102. Practice the law of positive attraction. You attract what you exhibit and model.

FINAL THOUGHTS

AT THE BEGINNING of our time together, I shared how, at times, serving others can fall to the wayside. I also extended an opportunity and challenge to use the timeless principles in this book to be of greater service to your family, friends, community, and world. My hope is that each of the principles highlighted will encourage you to grow in your thinking about service and enact several simple ways to serve daily. Furthermore, I hope you see yourself as an ambassador of these principles, paying it forward by encouraging others to serve – this is where your ability to empower others comes in.

My hope is that you will share this book, and the self-reflections at the end of each chapter, with others in your sphere of influence. I also hope that as you serve others, you continue to grow and prosper in your personal relationships, grow in business, and work relationships, and grow as an influencer in your community.

Just as important, I hope that you've picked at least one additional strategy to empower others from this book to enact into your life today. As you reflect on these final thoughts, I hope you will continue with your intentionality and develop a plan to serve and empower others. As part of your plan, please use the Equipped to Serve self-assessment, at

Equipped to Serve

the end of this section, to rate yourself on the defined principles. Once you rate yourself on implementing the principles, reflect and rate yourself according to which environment you are most likely to empower others. Once you complete your self-reflective rating, use the questions below to develop an intentional action plan to serve and empower others. Having the intention to serve others is wonderful, but I hope you'll leave our time together with a plan of action, so you can get to work changing the lives of your family, community, and the world today.

If you take nothing else from this work, I hope you'll take my father's words with you as I have taken them with me: "You never lose being kind."

Equipped to Serve Self-Assessment

EQUIPPED TO SERVE SELF ASSESSMENT Please score yourself using 1-7 scale with (7) beigh the highest score Next, chose the enviroment you are most comfortable completing this work								Which Environment Am I Likely to Empower Others		
	1	**2**	**3**	**4**	**5**	**6**	**7**	Home	Work	Community
Empower Others										
Quality-Time with Others										
Unselfishness Towards Others										
Inspire Others										
Positivity Towards Others										
People Centered										
Example For Others										
Develop Others										

Develop an intentional plan to Serve and Empower Others

- Develop a vision – what does serving others look like in your home, with relatives, at work and in your community? For example, my wife and I created a vision for our lives that included, "building businesses locally and serving our community."

Equipped to Serve

- What core values will drive your work and aid in helping you stay true to serving others? When the going gets tough, what is at your core?
- What three strategies will you apply to serve others? Will you focus on being a better parent by starting with better listening, or will you focus on living empowered to better support your work team?
- How will you measure your growth?

STAY CONNECTED - Visit www.jimmyhartglobal.com

Endnotes

1. Up from Slavery, Booker T. Washington, 1901
2. The New International Version Bible, Biblica, 1978
3. The 21 Irrefutable Laws of Leadership, Revised & Updated – 10th Anniversary Edition, John C. Maxwell, 2007
4. Livingston, Gretchen, and Kim Parker. "8 Facts about American Dads." Pew Research Center, 30 May 2020, www.pewresearch.org/fact-tank/2019/06/12/fathers-day-facts.
5. Ballard, Jamie. "Most Parents Wish They Were Having Family Dinners More Often." YouGov, 12 Nov. 2019, today.yougov.com/topics/lifestyle/articles-reports/2019/11/12/family-dinner-poll-survey.
6. "Why Inspiration Matters." Harvard Business Review, 21 Dec. 2021, hbr.org/2011/11/why-inspiration-matters.
7. "Positive Thinking: Stop Negative Self-Talk to Reduce Stress." Mayo Clinic, 3 Feb. 2022, www.mayoclinic.org/healthy-lifestyle/stress-management/in-depth/positive-thinking/art-20043950?reDate=21072022.
8. Vorel, Mike. "Seahawks Linebacker Shaquem Griffin Keeps Telling His Story so Kids like These Can Tell Theirs." The

Equipped to Serve

Seattle Times, 22 Nov. 2018, www.seattletimes.com/sports/seahawks/how-the-seahawks-rookie-linebacker-inspired-the-next-generation-of-shaquem-griffins.

9. Griffin, Shaquem, et al. Inseparable: How Family and Sacrifice Forged a Path to the NFL. Illustrated, Thomas Nelson, 2019.

10. "Nick Saban Coaching Tree: How Well Have His Assistants Fared?" Sports Illustrated, www.si.com/longform/2017/nick-saban-college-football-coaching-tree/index.html. Accessed 21 July 2022.

11. Taulbert, Clifton. Eight Habits of the Heart for Educators: Building Strong School Communities Through Timeless Values. 1st ed., Corwin, 2006.

12. Covey, Stephen. The Speed of Trust: The One Thing That Changes Everything. latest edition, 2022.

13. "Ansell: Helping Others Dampens the Effects of Everyday Stress." Yale School of Medicine, 14 Dec. 2015, medicine.yale.edu/news-article/ansell-helping-others-dampens-the-effects-of-everyday-stress.

14. Myers, Seth. "How to understand and handle bitter people." Psychology Today, Sussex Publishers, 7 Oct. 2019, https://www.psychologytoday.com/us/blog/insight-is-2020/201910/how-understand-and-handle-bitter-people

Made in the USA
Columbia, SC
06 March 2024